MESSIGRAPHICA

MESSIGRAPHICA

A GRAPHIC BIOGRAPHY OF THE GENIUS OF LIONEL MESSI

Sanjeev Shetty

For Laura, Raf and Ruben.
And Jimmy Forbes – the great survivor

Contents

Prologue   viii

1   The early years   01

2   Making a name for himself   17

3   Growing as a player – in a sinking ship   33

4   A Pep talk – and footballing greatness awaits   55

5   El Clásico – yes those ones   79

6   The main man versus the main man   91

7   La Albiceleste – talisman and tortured   105

8   Relax and rebirth   129

9   The champions again – of everything   145

10 Champions – again, and again and yet again   161

11 Back to the future   183

12 Where to now, young Leo?   201

13 Take your place, Leo – but where do you sit?   213

14 Being Messi brings its own rewards   225

15 Behind every great man   237

    Epilogue   248

    Picture and data credits   250

    Bibliography   251

    Acknowledgements   252

    Index   254

Prologue

'O jogo bonito' – the beautiful game

Let us not waste time about who said it first; the man we all associate with the phrase about the beautiful game is Pelé, the man that most people think is the best player who ever lived. Or at least, they did.

As I write this, I am forty-five. By the time you read it, another year will have been added to that number. The first footballer I can remember seeing is Kevin Keegan, the then European footballer of the year. I have seen Kenny Dalglish, John Barnes, Ryan Giggs, David Beckham, Paul Gascoigne and Marcelo Salas. I saw Steven Gerrard's first goal. Didier Drogba was pretty good, Fernando Torres was obviously iconic and Patrick Vieira glided across the grass like a leopard. And Thierry Henry was fast.

But I remember conversations I had during the first six or seven years of this century with Adnan Nawaz, then a sports presenter for BBC television, when we would debate who was the best player ever. He said Maradona, I said Pelé. But he had, as he tended to, the last word, when he mentioned a young player he had seen at Barcelona. He told me to watch out for him. The debate about who was the best player in the world was a regular one, but in recent times we have managed to reach agreement. But not on Pelé or Maradona.

Football likes are completely subjective. For instance, my favourite goal is the one scored by Carlos Alberto in the 1970 World Cup final. For anyone who will agree with me, there is another who will argue that the goal scored by Maradona in the 1986 World Cup was better. In the same way that we debate the greatest player ever – Maradona's incredible acceleration, close control and individual brilliance against Pelé's innovation and strength in the face of brutal man-marking – so our favourite games are also subjective and there are too many to debate or even mention briefly.

But the groundswell of current opinion suggests that Lionel Messi, aged twenty nine as I write this, is the best of all time. Why? Well, there are the numbers. More than five hundred career goals, two hundred assists and the all-time goals records for both Barcelona and Argentina. In the modern era, where numbers are prized above all else, Messi is the man who has forced his way to the top of any argument about who is the best.

But what is it that really makes a genius sportsman? What is the inner spark that creates the brilliance, the ability to score goals when it matters? For it is the goals that really tell the story. Those moments of individual brilliance that catapult a player beyond even the elite; the goals scored on the grandest stages and in title-winning matches. With Messi it is the goals he has scored in Champions League finals, Copa del Rey finals and the sheer volume against the most successful team in European football history, Real Madrid. The fact that he has managed to score a goal nearly every other game for Argentina, and has a hat-trick to his name against his nation's bitterest rivals, Brazil, speaks more than mere numbers.

But while statistics are great – after all, this book has more than a few of them – they do not account for one thing. Beauty. My wife tells me that Lionel Messi is a sweet-looking boy, but no more. But there is beauty and artistry in his feet. If you had never watched football before, you might wonder what all the fuss is about. But Messi's biggest talent is that he makes the seemingly impossible look ridiculously easy. And he seems to have done it for so long, I am feeling old just typing this.

We are fortunate to live in an era where sportsmen and women are performing regularly at the highest level. Serena Williams is almost certainly the greatest female tennis player. Roger Federer's claim to be the best man to hold a racket is similarly convincing. For more than a decade, Tiger Woods was the best golfer who ever lived. Usain Bolt ran so fast, it might be decades before anyone catches up. The All Blacks seem like the most complete rugby team the world has seen. Then we are back to football, and Lionel Messi.

You might ask, why write a book about him now? There are surely more chapters of his story still to be written. And you would be right. But this age is so fast, with technology changing by the minute, we might forget to do the things we are meant to do. Messi has already scored more goals than any other Barcelona player and he has broken the Primera División record. There are no more goalscoring feats he can achieve. He can only extend them. Better to chronicle what he has done and let it stand as a testament to what he has accomplished in a professional career little more than a decade old.

Hopefully, by reading this, you will find yourself lost in the images of a young boy, kicking a ball in his native Rosario, trying to prove that he is as good as his big brothers. Perhaps then you will remember why we love football: because at its best, it is so much fun. To play and also to watch. That young boy from Argentina grew up to be the best we have seen. I hope you will forgive me, Pelé.

* Where applicable, data is correct up until the end of the 2015–16 season, unless otherwise stated.

THE EARLY YEARS

1

A young man growing up in Rosario in central Argentina has no reason to believe his destiny is pre-ordained. An eclectic mix of musicians, poets, politicians and revolutionaries have all come from this typically humid part of South America. Where once its most famed resident was the Marxist revolutionary Che Guevara, its favourite son of the twenty-first century is a certain Lionel Andrés 'Leo' Messi. He was born on 24 June 1987, and rose to prominence for kicking around a football rather proficiently in the early days of the new Millennium.

Any child's future is shaped by those around them during their formative years. Young Leo, as he was known from an early age, had two football-mad older brothers. And cousins. And uncles. The Messis loved football and Leo could not avoid the family bug once he received his first ball at the age of three. Having finally convinced himself to take the present out into the street and play with it, rather than keep it for posterity, the young Messi began to nurture the talent that would bewitch a planet. It was around this time that he got the nickname 'La Pulga', which translated into English simply means 'The Flea'. The moniker probably came from one of his brothers and it referred, of course, to his size, or lack of. Plus the fact that no one could catch up with him once he was in full flight. His speed with the ball at his feet was something to behold even when he was at school. In matches they played when he was knee-high to a flea, it was the norm for him to score six or seven goals. You did not need to be a professional scout to spot the talent.

Despite his age and slight, underdeveloped frame, Messi played with boys much older than him on an abandoned military base. He was soon intoxicated with the game. In those days of the early 1990s, Argentina was towards the top of the football tree, having contested three World Cup finals in twelve years, winning two of them. The nation was united in the belief that it had the best player in the world in Diego Maradona. The popular notion is that because of their comparable physiques, Messi idolised Maradona. But young Leo was to harbour a love of playing so deep that Maradona was more a point of inspiration and achievement than a hero. Messi did not focus on being a certain player, he just wanted to be the best he could. At the age of

Lionel Messi *(third from the left, crouching down)* at age four and his coach Salvador Aparicio *(standing)*, with the children's football team of Club Grandoli.

The napkin on which the agreement for Leo's first Barcelona contract was written – 14 December 2000 was a big day for this serviette.

The early years

STARTING YOUNG

17

Lionel Messi was 17 years, 3 months and 22 days old when he featured in his first match for the senior side, the second-youngest player to ever wear the Blaugrana colours for the first team (the record holder is Paulino Alcántara).

16

Martina Hingis won the Australian Open tennis championship aged 16.

16

George Ford became the youngest professional rugby player in England in 2009 - aged 16 and 237 days.

14

Michelle Wie was 14 and nearly three months when she played in the 2004 Sony Open in Hawaii.

12

Mauricio Baldivieso, a striker for Aurora in the Bolivian league, was sent on as a 39th-minute substitute in a first division match against La Paz three days before his 13th birthday in 2009.

five he was playing football on a regular basis, joining his brothers in the street every day after school. It was the start of an obsession that lasts to this day. The only thing that may have stopped it was his over-protective brothers who tried to stop him playing with the older boys for fear that he would not be able to fight back when the going got rough. Messi dealt with those challenges with a shrug of the shoulders and did not worry about being kicked by anyone because 'the other boys would not be able to get the ball off me'. It showed that, even at such a tender age, he already had the natural confidence in his own ability that would underpin his career.

There was a curious aspect to Leo being so small: not only his family, but his peers and others around him were equally protective of him. He was, at times, both cheerful and cheeky. He showed early promise at school, in technical subjects like maths, but nothing could match his talent with a ball at his feet. Teachers were fairly sure that while his academic skills were improving, his thoughts were on the fields and playgrounds where the next ball would be kicked. Even at primary school, it was a given that you would win one of those playground games if Leo was on your team. Because he was so good, classmates, naturally, wanted to be his friend.

It is often said that although Messi has a strong attachment to his whole family, he felt the closest bond to his maternal grandmother. It was at her insistence that he took the place of a player who had not turned up for the local team, Grandoli. It was a family affair anyway: Messi Senior coached the team. Besides, it was a seven-a-side team so the conditions were not that threatening, and the other kids had already started to look out for him rather than kick him from pillar to post. Maybe they felt bad for him. As they all grew into bigger boys, Leo was still small, noticeably so.

There are no official statistics to say how common growth hormone deficiency is, but the chances of suffering from it are believed to be around one in 38,000. Leo was one of the ones. Even today doctors do not know enough to prevent it happening, but they are able to treat it. Messi was diagnosed with the condition at the age of eleven and was put on a course of treatment to help him grow. He told *The Daily Telegraph*: 'Every night I had to stick a needle into my legs, night after night after night, every day of the week, and this over a period of three years. I was so small, they said that when I went on to the pitch, or when I went to school, I was always the smallest of all. It was like this until I finished the treatment and I then started to grow properly.'

Even so, the treatment did not turn him into a giant, but it did allow him to grow at a normal rate. Some have speculated that the effect of HGH (Human Growth Hormone), which is a banned performance-enhancing drug for adults, may have given Messi an unfair advantage when it came to football. This was the verdict of the doctor who treated him, Diego Schwarsztein, who says the treatment given to the young Leo was still justified. He explained: 'The growth hormone has been used as a supplement by adults who do not need it, with the objective of gaining a sporting advantage. But you have to differentiate between growth hormone treatment for an adult who doesn't need it, who is looking for a physical benefit – and they are high doses and can have very negative side-effects – and the treatment of a physical deficiency in a young boy (like Messi).'

Leo's father, Jorge Messi, would have preferred to keep his son in Argentina. A trial with giants River Plate showcased the player's talents, but the difficulty was getting them to agree to contribute towards the HGH treatment. For the first two years of the treatment, Messi Senior had managed to find a way to pay for it, through state help and also from his own pocket. But the money was running out. With no agreement possible with River, the Messis were in limbo. But it was around this time that something else happened which would change the destiny of Lionel Messi's life. He was 'spotted'. A video of the young tyro during his trial with River had found its way to the experienced football agent Josep Maria Minguella. The only concern for Minguella was that he had never seen Messi play in the flesh, but even so an audition was set up for the boy at European giants Barcelona. He was just thirteen, and barely five feet tall, but his quality was immediately apparent. Barça's technical director at the time, Charly Rexach, was away at

The prizes have always been big for Leo, sometimes literally.

Messi takes a corner on his eigth birthday.

The early years

the Olympic Games in Sydney, and he was required to make the final judgment. So Messi was able to stay for more than a fortnight until Rexach's return, and continue to train with the club and its youngsters, who at this time included the likes of Cesc Fàbregas and Gerard Piqué. After seeing the young boy in a specially organised match at the Barcelona training camp, Rexach's mind was made up. 'We had to sign this kid right now. After two minutes, I knew', he would later say.

There were still obstacles to Messi becoming a Barcelona player. He had arrived in the city accompanied by his father, and if he was going to sign, Messi Senior would have to stay to act as chaperone. The club did offer Jorge Messi a job with a steady wage, as well as continuing his son's growth hormone treatment – courtesy of youth system administrator Joan Lacueva, who initially paid for the treatment out of his own pocket. But there were now other clubs interested in Leo's services. Real Madrid, for one, knew about this special teenager who had come from Argentina.

That Messi managed to cope with all the changes going on around him was probably because he hated losing. So much so that when the family played cards, the suspicion was that Leo would cheat. The disarming sight of such a little boy playing football against those much bigger than him should not obscure the fact that here was someone who already had a certainty over his ability. The difficulties settling in a new country would not interfere with his absolute determination to succeed. He could have been a River Plate player, but circumstances meant that he was now in Spain, on the books of one of the most famous clubs in the world.

The Messis had not yet committed to the club, although there was a feeling that Barcelona was the place they felt most comfortable. However, they were becoming twitchy about the lack of progress being made in putting a contract on the table. There was hesitation from Barcelona purely because of the player's age. He was still barely in his teens and there was no guarantee that the boy wonder would continue to develop as a player once he reached manhood. In the end there was a crunch meeting just before Christmas 2000 when Rexach

FIFA U20 World Cup
2005

6 / 7

Played six of seven games

6

Scored six goals

1

Voted best player of the tournament

Beijing Olympics
2008

5 / 6

Played five of six games

2

Scored two goals

1

Won gold medal

sat down with Minguella and the Messis and wrote down the basis for a contract on a restaurant napkin. Although there would be more nervous moments along the way, a year later Messi would sign another contract and underline how determined he was to make a life for himself in Catalonia.

Rexach's enthusiasm and confidence in sealing the deal was quickly rewarded. This was no slow burner. Messi would prove himself at all five internal levels on his way to the first team. It was Frank Rijkaard, the man who had played with the likes of Ruud Gullit, Marco van Basten and Dennis Bergkamp, and who was now entrusted with ending a barren spell for the Catalans, who gave Messi his chance with the established players. Messi had been working his way through the Cadete, Juvenil A, Juvenil B, Barcelona C and Barcelona B teams since 2000, when the Dutchman asked for a bunch of 'kids' to make up the numbers in a friendly match in 2003. Those kids included Messi. From November 2003, fast forward nearly twelve months to his first-team debut against local rivals Espanyol. It was only as a substitute, but eyebrows were raised when he came on in the eighty-second minute to replace the established Deco. He was not even on the pitch long enough to receive a rating from the local newspaper, but the boy who was fast becoming a man in footballing terms said it was ten minutes he would never forget.

It was not uncommon for young Argentines to fly the nest and seek their football destinies away from the homeland. Normally, though, these wannabee professionals would go on their own, and had little contact with their family. Where Messi's story is different is that his father was a close and protective influence that has never disappeared. It was not that Jorge Messi was an archetypal pushy parent; he had the vision and sensed that his son was truly a special talent. Perhaps it was Leo's pure love for the game that was the key. Messi Senior simply took his little boy on a journey because that was what seemed to make young Leo happy. He was happiest when he was kicking a ball all day, whether it was in training or playing. When he was smaller, Leo used to go to sleep with a football. Rumour has it that he still does.

So much of sport is down to fate. In 1995, the English Premier League champions Blackburn Rovers could afford to splash out to retain their position at the top. But their chairman Jack Walker decided he did not need to strengthen central midfield, and rejected the suggestion that they should recruit an unknown called Zinedine Zidane, then playing for Bordeaux in France. 'Why do we want to sign Zidane when we have Tim Sherwood?' has gone down in the annals of memorable quotes.

Similarly, in 2001, Jon McLeish was just another young man obsessed with the computer game Football Manager. One of the options available to him was to select a player in the Barcelona team called Lionel Messi, even though he had yet to make his debut in real life. As the computerised version of the player began to rack up the goals, the teenaged Jon told his father of Messi's achievements. His dad was Alex McLeish, then manager of Glasgow Rangers. With plenty on his plate, the Scot thanked his son for the information and carried on regardless.

What makes this story even more pertinent is that three years later, before Messi had made his first-team bow, McLeish made inquiries about whether there were any youngsters Rangers could take on loan from Barcelona. Messi and Andrés Iniesta were mentioned as possible candidates. However, both clubs decided that the physical nature of Scottish football would bring too many potential risks for the young men. So Messi and Iniesta stayed in Spain and never graced the Scottish Premier League.

HOW DOES MESSI MEASURE UP?

Professional athletes are primed to physical perfection – side by side their vital statistics make for interesting comparison. Messi, one of the smaller players in professional football, is also the lightest – helping to earn him the nickname 'The Flea'. Here Messi's BMI is measured against fellow players and elite sportsmen.

22.1

22.6

23.4

Gareth Bale

Height: 1.83m / 6ft
Weight: 74kg / 11.7st
BMI: 22.1

Novak Djokovic

Height: 1.88m / 6ft 2in
Weight: 80kg / 12.6st
BMI: 22.6

Cristiano Ronaldo

Height: 1.85m / 6ft 1in
Weight: 80kg / 12.6st
BMI: 23.4

24.0

25.5

27.5

Lionel Messi

Height: 1.7m / 5ft 7in
Weight: 67kg / 10.6st
BMI: 24.0

Wayne Rooney

Height: 1.76 / 5ft 9in
Weight: 83kg / 13.1st
BMI: 25.5

LeBron James

Height: 2.03m / 6ft 8in
Weight: 113kg / 17.9st
BMI: 27.5

The early years

MAKING
A NAME
FOR HIMSELF

2

**IN MY ENTIRE LIFE I HAVE
NEVER SEEN A PLAYER
OF SUCH QUALITY AND
PERSONALITY AT SUCH A
YOUNG AGE.**

Fabio Capello

It is easy to forget how much the modern Barcelona owes to the innovation, skill and sheer wit of Ronaldinho. The Brazilian transformed the Catalans from a side living in the shadow of Real Madrid into repeat champions of Spain and Europe. In 2005, he was at his peak, prompting, dictating, scoring and creating. His stellar form was the catalyst behind Barça ending six barren seasons without winning La Liga, a title they had won six times during the 1990s.

On 1 May, relegation-bound Albacete came to Camp Nou. The champions-elect were leading by a solitary Samuel Eto'o goal. But with a distinct nervousness in the air, a second goal was required to put the ninety thousand-plus supporters at ease. Head coach Frank Rijkaard elected to substitute Eto'o for Messi. The newcomer had a goal disallowed within seconds of entering the fray, and the game was drifting into injury time with Barcelona still searching for the second goal to put an exclamation mark on their evening. The second goal did come and predictably the man at the heart of the move was Ronaldinho. The threat he posed meant that every time he received the ball five defenders immediately surrounded him. So, when he received the ball centrally maybe forty yards from goal, he was again mobbed by Albacete defenders. But the playmaker was so gifted that teammate Eidur Gudjohnsen joked that he could 'make the ball talk'. At that moment, Ronaldinho looked left to see a chunky kid sprinting ahead. The pass had to be played quickly to avoid the offside trap that had caught them out numerous times already that night. It was lobbed into the boy's path. He was maybe twelve yards from goal, with just the goalkeeper to beat. The ball was bouncing and needed volleying, not the easiest opportunity for a seventeen year old. But with a flash of his soon-to-be-celebrated left boot, the ball was in the net.

'Messi! Remember the name', yelled the Sky Sports commentator Rob Palmer as the boy from Rosario claimed his first senior goal for Barça. Sometimes the man behind the mic takes a chance and hopes that events in the future bear out his perception. Or sometimes there is enough evidence already to suggest that a bit of speculation might be worth it. 'We knew he was coming through and we knew he was going to have an instant impact', says Palmer, who has commentated on Spanish football for more than twenty years and has seen other prodigious talents emerge, including Cristiano Ronaldo and Luís Figo.

There would be more goals to follow in the months ahead, although Messi would be injured at the moment Barcelona proved they were the best team in Europe at the end of the 2005–06 season by beating Arsenal in the Champions League final. However, an off-the-cuff comment from one of his teammates would further enhance the legend. Ronaldinho had just received the Ballon d'Or in 2005 when he announced: 'This award says I'm the best player in the world, but I'm not even the best player at Barcelona. Since he began to come and train with us we knew we would go down this path. Someday I will explain that I was at the birth of one of the footballing greats: Leo Messi.'

Messi had signed his first senior professional contract at the start of his breakthrough season, having turned eighteen. In Spain, as in most European countries, players have a buyout clause that can offer a clue of how highly they are valued by their club. Messi's was set at a staggering 150 million euros. But the secret was already out. Messi had starred in a pre-season game against Italian opposition. Juventus, with Fabio Capello as manager, had made moves to take him on loan, while another Italian giant, Inter Milan, were willing to part with hard cash to sign him. Still in his impressionable teenage years, Messi's head was nearly turned. His Argentina teammate Juan Sebastián Verón, confirmed in 2015 that the young man was keen on the move. Joan Laporta, the Barcelona president at the time, recalls it as the closest that Messi came to leaving. It did not happen, although the talk continued around him. Barcelona's pre-season game (footage of his exploits remains on the club's official website) developed such a buzz around Messi that he became almost as big a conversation point as the club itself.

Capello, the future England manager, was moved to say: 'I saw him playing for the Argentina youth team, and he looked like a good player. But it's something else to see him in this stadium, in that shirt

TEENAGE KICKS – THE PROFESSIONAL DEBUTS

In comparison with other greats of the game, Lionel
Messi achieved plenty of his footballing firsts before
he was out of his teenage years.

Lionel Messi

Pelé

	Lionel Messi				Pelé			
15 yrs old							●	
16 yrs old								
17 yrs old	●	●			●	●	●	●
18 yrs old	●	●						
19 yrs old								
20 yrs old								
21 yrs old	●					●	●	
22 yrs old	●							
23 yrs old								
24 yrs old								
25 yrs old								
26 yrs old								
27 yrs old								

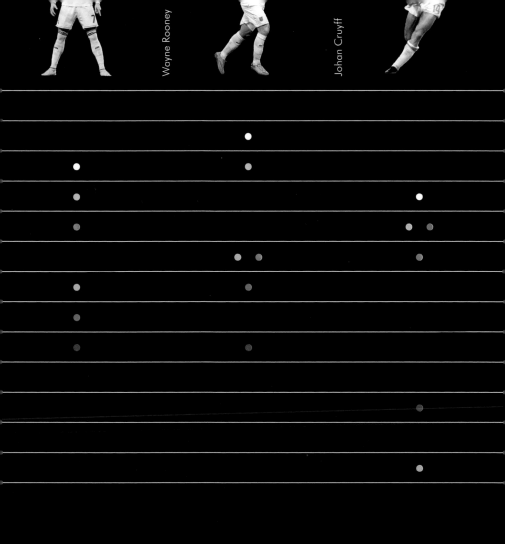

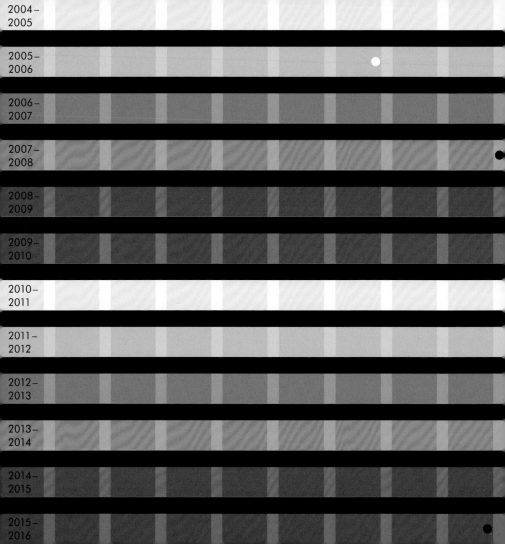

2004–
2005

2005–
2006

2006–
2007

2007–
2008

2008–
2009

2009–
2010

2010–
2011

2011–
2012

2012–
2013

2013–
2014

2014–
2015

2015–
2016

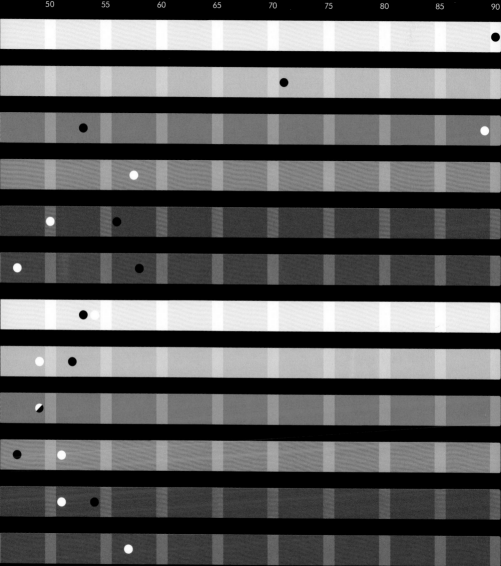

and before so many people… In my entire life I have never seen a player of such quality and personality at such a young age, particularly wearing the "heavy" shirt of one of the world's great clubs.'

Messi's 2005–06 season would ultimately be curtailed by injury, so his statistics in isolation do not make particularly impressive reading. But the proof was in the watching. He made just seventeen appearances in the Primera División that season, scoring six times. Playing from a more fixed right-wing position than the freer role in which he now operates, Messi did not have as many chances to shoot as he would now, having just thirty-two attempts on goal. It was a different story in the Champions League. He played in six games, scored once but was happy to try his luck more often, with twenty shots at an average of more than three a game. The flipside to being labelled a prodigy is that opponents try to stop you by fair means or foul. In a last-sixteen tie against Chelsea, the Spaniard Asier del Horno was shown a red card for a series of uncompromising challenges. 'It was already obvious from his first attack on me that he went in really to kick me on the knee', said Messi after the game. It was a defining moment: an acknowledgement that this would be something he would have to get used to.

In years to come, Messi's post-match utterances became few and far between, and he would rarely complain about some of the rough treatment he received. For observers, the hypnotic nature of his performance left an indelible mark. One tribute came from the respected writer James Lawton in the *Independent*: 'Messi's supreme quality is an ability to cover the ground with bewildering surges of intricate pace. The great tribute to George Best was that he bestowed twisted blood on hard-pressed defenders. The same effect was experienced by the agonised left flank of Chelsea's defence. One of them was sent to the dressing room. The rest of them could have only have felt profound envy.'

The moment the comparisons start is the time when people begin to pay attention. What was significant was that Messi was shining in a team full of stars. This Barcelona team featured Samuel Eto'o, Ronaldinho, Deco and Thiago Motta, with substitutes of the calibre of

Andrés Iniesta and Henrik Larsson. Yet all these big names were overshadowed by the Argentine. His mercurial rise was soon to be cut short by injury. In the second leg of the tie against Chelsea, he tore muscle fibres in his right thigh and lasted just twenty-five minutes. He was to aggravate the problem further in training. It was easy to imagine that such injuries would plague the career of someone whose ability seemed freakish. In comparison to most players he was still small, despite the growth hormone treatment, and yet he was able to produce so many moments of speed, power and finesse, suggesting a body that was working at its very limit. If it was not the thigh muscle, then surely the hamstring was vulnerable. With the modern boots that are built for speed rather than protection, his metatarsals faced a higher risk than other players'.

Barcelona completed the job of winning the Champions League without Leo, who had not played in the two and a half months since the Chelsea game. In his mind, although he received a medal for his part in getting Barça to the final, he did not feel worthy of the prize. The sombre look on his face in the pictures taken during the team's celebrations after the 2–1 win against Arsenal emphasise just what a difficult time it was for a player still in his teens whose eagerness had been stopped by injury.

It was doubly unfortunate for Messi that the injury should fall in a World Cup year. The summer of 2006 was supposed to be the opportunity for the world to see for itself the phenomenon that was regularly dazzling Spain. Messi had yet to establish himself as a fixture in the Argentina national side, but having already tasted success with his club he was thinking ahead to what could be an incredible climax to his season.

Messi's arrival in international football had not mirrored the fairytale start to his club career. He had been played as a substitute in a less-than-friendly game against Hungary on 17 August 2005. Entering the pitch in the sixty-third minute, he should in theory have enjoyed a twenty-seven-minute debut. Instead, he managed just two. While trying to evade the attentions of a tactile defender, he used his arm to fend off

Making a name for himself

the opponent. The referee chose to interpret the act as violent and showed a straight red card. Messi was reduced to tears.

Although he would start for his country in the following months, and also score his first goal in a friendly against Croatia, he was by no means at the forefront of José Pékerman's thoughts when the World Cup in Germany came round. The coach may well have been influenced by the thigh injury that had troubled Messi since March.

Twenty years had passed since Argentina's last World Cup triumph, that glorious month in Mexico in 1986 when Diego Maradona entranced the world. Expectation among the South American side's supporters and media had again risen to fever pitch. This was a side full of talent, from the wily central defender Roberto Ayala through to the clinical striker Hernán Crespo. Most of the squad plied their trade away from their homeland, and their prospects of success were seen as strong. Sufficiently strong that the fact Messi was not an automatic choice provided a topic of discussion, but not a vociferous argument. During a searing 6–0 demolition of Serbia and Montenegro in their second group game, Messi scored and created another goal after being introduced as a substitute. The decision by the coach to use him sparingly was vindicated: at international level Messi decorated games at this stage, but was not ready to dictate. The answer to the question about where Messi would fit in Pékerman's plans was put on hold. For Barcelona, he nominally played from the right wing, with licence to drift into the centre, either to make goals or to score them. For Argentina, he was being groomed as a more than able deputy for Juan Román Riquelme, who enjoyed a free role, akin to the 'false number nine' that Messi would go on to play for Barça.

The South American football expert Tim Vickery, writing for the BBC, noted after Messi had become the youngest Argentine to feature in a World Cup: 'Watching Messi it was hard to escape the conclusion that his long-term future lies in the centre, rather than stuck out on the wing. It is where most of the truly great players operate – like, for example, Messi's two most illustrious compatriots, Diego Maradona and Alfredo di Stéfano.'

The victory over Serbia and Montenegro meant Argentina had qualified for the knockout stages of the tournament with a game to spare. Messi was afforded a start in the next match, the dead rubber against Holland. He would last just sixty-nine minutes of that goalless draw, marked out of the match by the uncompromising Khalid Boulahrouz. He would come on during the extra-time victory over Mexico in the round-of-sixteen, but would play no part in Argentina's final game, a penalty-shoot-out defeat in the quarter-final by the hosts Germany. Although Messi was on the bench, coach Pékerman opted to use other substitutes, favouring the bruising striker Julio Cruz over his little technician.

Major tournaments are a tough baptism for any young player with the squad dynamic and the fact the eyes of the world and a prying press make their lives almost unlivable for four weeks. Even more so when the squad enters that tournament with expectations and leaves in the cruellest way possible. Messi's football education would continue and the harsh lessons would become more frequent over the next few seasons, lessons that ultimately would push him to develop tactically and technically and adapt to his compatriots.

Pahiño
Manuel Badenes
Làszló Kubala

Cristiano Ronaldo

Ferenc Puskàs

11

30

12

Lionel Messi

Isidro Làngara

13

26

16

22

César Rodriguez

19

Alfredo Di Stéfano
Telmo Zarra

Edmundo Suàrez

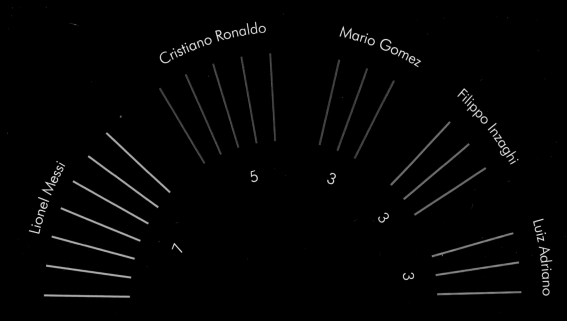

Cristiano Ronaldo

Mario Gomez

Filippo Inzaghi

Lionel Messi

Luiz Adriano

5

3

7

3

3

Messi's career hat-tricks: 41
Barcelona: 37
Argentina: 4
29 Feb 2012 v Switzerland
09 Jun 2012 v Brazil
14 Jun 2013 v Guatemala
10 Jun 2016 v Panama

Ronaldo's career hat-tricks: 42
4 for Portugal, 1 Man Utd, 37 Real Madrid

Most hat-tricks in a career
Pelé: 92 hat-tricks

Making a name for himself

GROWING AS A PLAYER – IN A SINKING SHIP

3

'

I HAVE SEEN THE PLAYER WHO WILL INHERIT MY PLACE IN ARGENTINE FOOTBALL AND HIS NAME IS MESSI. MESSI IS A GENIUS AND HE CAN BECOME AN EVEN BETTER PLAYER. HIS POTENTIAL IS LIMITLESS AND I THINK HE'S GOT EVERYTHING IT TAKES TO BECOME ARGENTINA'S GREATEST PLAYER.

'

Diego Maradona in February 2006

If Barcelona had been governed by the code of *omertà*, where no one could go on the record and herald the future best player in the world, it was becoming harder to keep the secret to themselves. One day in the future, Maradona would make some less charitable comments about Lionel Messi, but his words of praise after the match against Chelsea at Stamford Bridge were taken at face value. The comparisons between the two were inevitable: both were speedy, stocky dribblers with a vision of where teammates were around them, and a certainty in their own ability to start or end moves.

In the last twenty years, Barcelona have produced a number of great teams who all have one thing in common: a shelf life. Each team starts life as a winning machine, even if the beauty is so overwhelming that you hardly notice how efficient it is. The team that Messi broke into was largely dependent on one player: Ronaldinho. But the mercurial Brazilian had peaked. For two years, he had been the best player in the world, but now injuries, loss of form and, arguably, lack of dedication, were taking their toll. At his best, he dictated the way Barcelona played and had led them to two La Liga titles and only the second Champions League triumph in their history. The former Superman of the Primera División began to play as if kryptonite was attached to his formerly twinkling toes. As he plummeted, so too did the stock of manager Frank Rijkaard. Barcelona began to struggle both domestically and internationally. Even worse, the *Galacticos* at Real Madrid were finally getting their act together. Zinedine Zidane and David Beckham departed the Bernabéu as players with the league title in their hands. In contrast, Messi and cohorts ended the season empty-handed, with the exception of the Spanish Super Cup, won at the start of the campaign.

The boy king was still only nineteen, but with chaos beginning to envelop Barcelona, he carried the hope for the future. Fitness, though, was still an issue. His growing body was vulnerable to developing serious injuries consistent with men in sport of that age group. In the middle of November 2006, Messi was struck down by the dreaded metatarsal injury. The eighty-seven days he spent recovering was the longest time he spent away from the field before or since. Up to that point, the Camp Nou faithful were seeing what they had been promised and had now come to expect. Although Ronaldinho had been their main man for three seasons, and had been a significant instigator in bringing the quiet, young Messi into the players' inner circle, it was the Argentine who was giving the supporters hope that another generation of dominance would follow.

Despite the hiatus caused by the metatarsal injury, the 2006–07 season would be memorable for two major Messi moments. The first was a hat-trick against Real Madrid in the latter stages of the season in front of his own fans. Both sides were licking their wounds after being knocked out of the Champions League, but Real had high hopes of ending a four-year drought without a trophy by winning the Primera División. On a raucous evening, Real struck first. Messi equalised. Real scored again. Messi scored Barcelona's second. Madrid got a third. Then, in injury time, Messi's status as a club legend was assured. Writing in the *Guardian*, Spanish football expert Sid Lowe said: 'An epic hat-trick against Real Madrid showed that the 473rd New Maradona is worth every last drop of hype.' Lowe was referring to the previous players who had been unjustifiably compared to the great man. Now, though, the heir apparent had been revealed. The praise rang out from all and sundry with Samuel Eto'o saying: 'Messi is above any other player. He has another gear.'

Like the best athletes in any sport, Messi makes everything look simple. His goals that night, though, were anything but. For his first, he collected the ball from Eto'o twenty yards from goal. He had drifted in from the right and was now unmarked. The pass was weighted perfectly and Messi's first touch took the ball out of his feet and allowed him to approach the Real goal with a choice of finishes. He could go to Iker Casillas's left or right. The Spaniard, arguably the best goalkeeper in the world at the time, waited for Messi to make his move. The clue he thought he spotted indicated Messi would go to his left. He spread himself to dive that way. Messi chose instead to drive a left-footed shot to Casillas's right. Upon scoring, Messi lifted his shirt to reveal a dedication to his uncle, who had just lost his father (*Fuerza, tio* –

strength, uncle). Then he celebrated with Eto'o, his delight, exuberance and adrenalin showing that he knew a goal against Real was worth more than most.

For the second, the assist came from Ronaldinho. Those feet were dancing this time as he raided down the Real right, beating three defenders before shooting from eight yards. Casillas saved, but the loose ball fell to Messi. Casillas was no longer guarding the goal, but a Real defender was and two more were getting into position. The ball was off the ground, but with remarkable precision and power Messi volleyed it into the right corner. Parity was Barcelona's again.

With league leaders Sevilla having lost earlier, victory was key to both sides. Real had not been top all season, but now carried menace and genuine desire. Barcelona were down to ten men following the sending-off of Oleguer and in the second half went 3–2 behind when a young Sergio Ramos scored. In search of yet another equaliser, Barcelona risked being punished on the counter. With time almost up, they still drove on. The decisive move was once again started by Ronaldinho, who cut in from the left, almost begging for someone to make a run that he could pick out. Thirty yards from goal, Messi made a slight move from right of centre. The ball found him and his first touch made all the difference. It took him from centre to the left and invited a challenge from a tired Real defender. Iván Helguera was left on the floor as Messi poked the ball past him. Three touches were all that were required to take him past a clutch of defenders and home in on goal. He was to the left of the goal. Again Casillas stood in his way. On this occasion, the goalkeeper had a slight advantage because Messi had to go to his left. Besides, no one in world football had a better set of reflexes that equipped them to stop shots. In Messi's mind was the knowledge that he had shown the keeper his hand. He had already scored with a sidefoot and then a blasted shot. What else did he have in his locker? How about this? Messi shot to the keeper's left, making the ball rise and then dip with power. Casillas dived but in vain. And he stayed down, the pain refusing to abate. On the sideline, the Real manager Fabio Capello looked to the skies for some form of message.

On average, Messi is fouled twice in a game, so riding
tackles is nearly as important as avoiding them.

Growing as a player – in a sinking ship

The only hope he might have received was that the game was nearly over and Messi could do no more damage.

That mad March night was the moment that Messi lived up to the hype, the night the football landscape changed forever. The game had plenty of stars – Thierry Henry, Didier Drogba, Kaka and a young Cristiano Ronaldo to name but a few – and yet Messi was just nineteen and had done something that no footballer had achieved in twelve years – to score three times in a Real–Barça game. At first, the discussions about Messi might have been about what sort of player he was: was he a winger, a playmaker or even a striker? They were fast becoming irrelevant. He was simply a winner.

The football world was still catching its breath when Messi wrote another chapter in his embryonic story. The comparisons to Maradona were now too obvious to ignore. In that final equaliser against Real, there were shades of the goal Maradona scored against Belgium in the 1986 World Cup. But no one could score a goal like the one he scored against England. Could they? If Maradona's second goal in the quarter-final in the high altitude of Mexico City is not the greatest goal ever scored, then it is at least in the top two. The sight of Maradona gliding past England defenders at will before aiming his shot into the corner of the net was perhaps even more iconic than the sight of him holding aloft the World Cup at the end of the tournament. It remains a reference point for a career that some claim to be the greatest of them all. It was a goal surely no one could equal, let alone eclipse. That was until Lionel Messi came on the scene.

To go back more than twenty years previously, Maradona was dominating the World Cup and had just given Argentina the lead with a goal that at first sight looked like a header, but was revealed by slow-motion replays as a very deliberate handball. While those watching on television were still trying to digest what they had just seen, no one was anticipating the danger that lurked around the corner as Maradona picked up the ball inside his own half, surrounded by England players…

Now, in April 2007, on a hot night at Camp Nou, in a Copa del Rey semi-final against Getafe, Messi picked up the ball in a similar corner of the pitch (right side, five yards from the halfway line). He had two players to beat almost immediately. Like Maradona before him, he did that with assuredness and confidence, but he was still fifty yards from goal. Already trailing in his wake were Javier Paredes and Nacho Perez. 'I could have fouled him at that point, but I didn't think it was a good option because it would have cost me a yellow card, and I never thought he would do what he did,' said Paredes in an interview eight years later. Like the ninety thousand at the stadium, he could not predict what would happen next. But back to Mexico.

Maradona had left two vanquished English opponents, Peter Beardsley and Peter Reid, with ringside views as his stocky legs galloped and glided away across the turf. The fact that he was running at such speed and beating players meant the fact that the ball appeared to be tied to his ankles went unnoticed. Around forty yards out from the goal, he beat a third man. Still he dribbled with his left foot dominant.

Meanwhile, in Barcelona, Messi had gone to top speed, also sprinting past a third man, beating him with pace, not trickery. He, too, had the goal in his sights. At this stage he must surely have wondered whether to pass the ball to someone better placed or carry on. He had already beaten three men and just two central defenders remained.

Maradona was faced with a similar problem: yes, he could have passed, and as a player with both creative and killer instincts he was not governed by selfishness. Indeed, there is a story that Maradona apologised to one of his teammates for not passing, acknowledging that he was aware of his presence, but the pass would have been too difficult to make. When Maradona beat his third man, he had just one more defender to beat. He cut round to his right, taking him further away from goal. The England goalkeeper, Peter Shilton, came out to challenge and Maradona cut to the right again. To finish the move required the most acute of finishes. But the great players worry less about what they cannot do – they strive when no one is watching to make themselves better. With his body falling to the floor, Maradona managed to use his left foot to strike the ball into an empty net.

IN THE RIGHT PLACE

While still a teenager, Messi played on the right-hand side for Barcelona, but his desire to play through the middle was obvious. As highlighted here, he spends nearly a quarter of his time in the middle of the opponent's half. Ten years on and he has returned to the right, spending more than half his playing time on the right-hand flank, either in his, or the opponent's half. His pitch coverage and movement has become more disciplined, though this has rendered him no less effective.

2006/2007

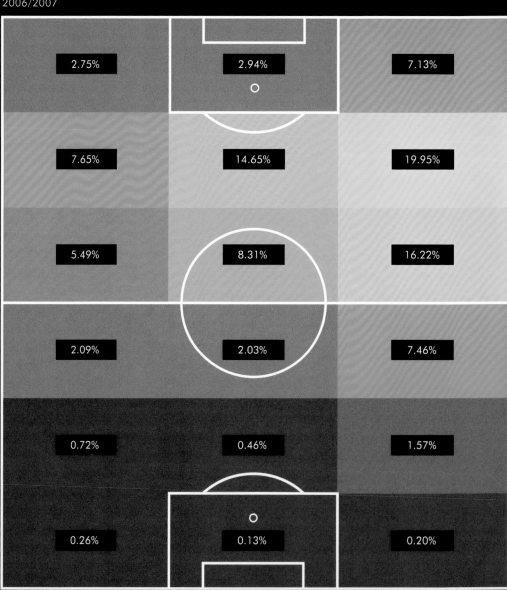

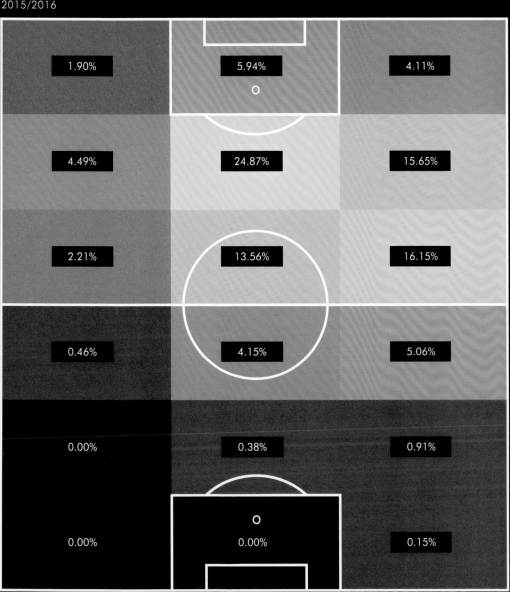

The sprint speed of some of football's fastest forwards.
All speeds recorded at the players' optimal level.

29.40 kmph
18.27 mph

31.20 kmph
19.4 mph

32.50 kmph
20.19 mph

Neymar

Rooney

Messi

33.60kmph
20.80mph

34.70kmph
21.56mph

35.10kmph
21.80mph

Ronaldo

Bale

Valencia

Against Getafe, Messi also chose to dribble to his right. Five defenders had tried to stop him and failed. The goalkeeper forced Messi to go further right. At the time no one really knew how good Messi's right foot was. Now they found out. Messi ran towards the corner flag, and at that point everyone realised they had seen the goal before. Right down to the celebration. The modern colour televisions might shine more brightly, but the images nearly twenty years apart are otherwise the same. 'It was the best goal I have ever seen in my life', said Deco. Barcelona's sporting director, Txiki Begiristain, was even more effusive: 'I hope Maradona can forgive me, but I think Messi's goal is even better.'

In the Spanish paper *AS*, Alfredo Relaño compared Messi to Elmyr de Hory, the forger of famous paintings who always put his signature upside down. 'So, you can copy a work of art, after all', he wrote. 'This was a replica, with the same path, the same acceleration with every touch, the same pauses and feints, always escaping on the same side. The only difference was Messi finishing with his right foot – that was the upside-down signature.'

When Messi scored that goal, Maradona did not see it. Not because he did not want to, but because he was caught in the middle of a downward spiral of alcohol abuse, addiction to cocaine and chronic obesity. He was quite literally fighting for his life. The legend, though, was in Messi's thoughts. He dedicated the goal to the man who did more than anyone to put Argentina on the map. At the same time Messi also made a rare disclosure on his vision of how he played. 'I wait for the defender's movement', he said. 'I play with him. Once I see what he does, I feint to go one way, then go the other. I keep looking at my opponent's feet, not the ball. I know where the ball is. I know it is there.'

However, perhaps as much as the goal showed that Messi was heading towards superstardom, it would also indicate that Barcelona were in danger of hitting a plateau. On the night, they beat Getafe 5–2. But this was a two-legged tie, and they lost the second leg 4–0. The wonder goal would ultimately count for nothing. Just another addition to the Messi highlights reel. Further disappointment would follow for Messi that summer in the colours of Argentina.

The Copa América is the Southern Hemisphere's equivalent to the European Championship, though it is only contested by teams from South and Central America. The 2007 tournament was held in Venezuela and there was a sense before it started that the winner would be either Brazil or Argentina. Messi's men won all their three group games, scoring nine goals. They were no less impressive in the knockout stages, putting four past Peru and dismantling the dangerous Mexicans 3–0. There was an irresistible nature to Argentina's football. The blend of experience – Gabriel Heinze, Juan Román Riquelme and Roberto Ayala – married to the youthful talents of Javier Mascherano and Messi, made them popular among neutrals. Messi, now at the grand age of twenty, had scored in both the quarter and semi-final.

The Argentine style was patient, probing passing, something that Messi would get used to under future managers at Camp Nou. But it could be disrupted by raw aggression and power. Brazil proved that in the final, taking an early lead and then breaking up Argentina's rhythm. Beaten 3–0, Messi left the tournament with nothing but a runners-up medal and the memory of one of the best goals. In the semi-final against Mexico, he played ostensibly as a left winger. It was not until the sixty-first minute, with his side 1–0 to the good, that he finally shook off the limpet-like man-marking and found some space. He was on the Argentina right, twenty yards from goal, with one defender just in front of him. With the ball under his control, he spotted Oswaldo Sánchez slightly off his goal-line. The chip-lob was not an obvious finish for anyone, and had not yet been seen as part of Messi's wide-ranging repertoire. But with the most delicate of movements, he lifted the ball into the net and his country into the final. However, it would be his last significant contribution to the tournament.

The start of the following season was marked by the arrivals of Thierry Henry and the Ivorian Yaya Touré at Camp Nou. The French international was in the twilight of his top-flight career, yet it was those players coming to the end of their duties who made the difference.

Oh look – he's scored again.
Just don't stop when you get to 600.

Ronaldinho was very nearly done: he had started the previous season as the role-maker of the side and ended it as a man without an obvious future. With Ronaldinho being phased out, the most obvious man to fill his shoes was Messi. With Henry arriving, and Samuel Eto'o now firmly established as one of the mainstays of the side, the front three picked themselves. But, among them, they only started 101 games. In a season where Barça reached the semi-finals of the Champions League, all three players would normally have been expected to start forty games each. But there was a sense of chaos about Barcelona. Rijkaard was at the end of his tether and any notion that he could rely on Messi to be his main man, and save him from the enveloping crisis, was undermined by two injuries. The first was a thigh injury just fourteen days before the end of 2007; the second in March was captured beautifully by Hugo Steckelmacher, the British-born, Barcelona-based writer.

He wrote: 'The stage is FC Barcelona's famous Camp Nou stadium. The scoreline? 1–0, although you'd be forgiven for thinking that no one cared. The reason for this lack of interest? One of the divo's [sic] clothed in red and blue is prostrated pitchside, tears streaming down his youthful face. The moment is frozen in time. Thousands of fans hold their hearts in their hands. A legendary Dutch player, now FC Barcelona manager, looks down at the ground. After just thirty-five minutes of a Champions League second-leg tie, suddenly Europe's premier club competition doesn't seem so important any more. As Nietzsche once wrote, "God is dead"; and in this case, Lionel Messi lies injured yet again.'

This latest setback would keep him out for five weeks, but the bigger concern was that he had already suffered seven muscle injuries in his brief career. He was only twenty; this was not a grizzled veteran coming to the end of his playing days. Rijkaard had maybe recognised that Messi's body was becoming fragile because of the large number of games he had played at such a young age; he had chosen to rest him a week earlier from the 4–2 defeat by Atlético Madrid. Howls of derision from Barça fans may have made Rijkaard rethink, but his problems were manifest. Half his squad had suffered injuries in the past two seasons, hinting at a serious issue with the team's fitness. Significantly, there was a noticeable drop-off in Messi's performances after the sixty-minute mark, suggesting below-average training and preparation. As Messi tried to learn and adapt to his adult body, the Argentina national team doctor Homero de Agostino explained at the time: 'What he asks of himself is too much … he wants to kick every ball, to be involved in every move, to score every goal. If when running one does more than one really can, at some point the muscle is fatigued, coordination between the contraction and relaxation of the muscle is offset by a millisecond, and an injury occurs.'

The discussion around Messi's frequent injury problems led some to speculate that he might never reach his potential. The Barcelona media asked questions of everything about him: why was he always injured, was he being played too much, did he need to be rested? This after all was a player who was being seen increasingly as Barça's talisman. Perhaps an even better measure of where he was, and where he could go, was seen at the Bernabéu where the extremely talented Dutchman Arjen Robben was continually plagued by hamstring injuries. Robben was seldom rested either at his former club Chelsea or by Real Madrid, the need for his unique skills over-riding thoughts that his long-term future might hinge on more careful management of his fragile hamstrings. Messi was no different. Played at almost every juncture, with his body suggesting that his frame could snap at any point, meant there was plenty of scepticism about whether his career would ever scale the hoped-for pinnacles. Indeed, Steckelmacher suggested that Messi was heading for the same fate as Marco van Basten, another terrific talent who was overplayed before retiring at the age of twenty-eight through chronic injury. 'All of the signs point to Messi suffering similar problems', he wrote.

By the time Messi had recovered, there was a sense that Barcelona were approaching the end of an era. They were some distance off the pace in the Primera División, and in the Champions League they had been drawn against Manchester United in the semi-finals. A 0–0 draw in the first leg at Camp Nou was followed by an equally cagey second leg at Old Trafford where a solitary goal from United midfielder Paul Scholes settled the tie. What threat Barça posed came from Messi. But they had not yet found a way to stop intelligent defences crowding out their diminutive attacker. United went on to win European football's most important prize. There would be future meetings between the two sides, and Messi would not lose any of them.

Barcelona finished the season in third place in the domestic league, a full eighteen points behind champions Real Madrid. In addition to their Champions League exit, they also went out in the semi-final of the Copa del Rey. On 8 May 2008, the club announced that Rijkaard would step down after five seasons to be replaced by Catalan legend Pep Guardiola. The former midfielder had been coach of the Barcelona B side for just one season, and although results had been impressive, this was considered a largely uninspired appointment. The young coach immediately made it clear that Ronaldinho, Deco and Samuel Eto'o were not part of his plans. It was an announcement that suggested an air of ruthlessness sweeping through Camp Nou at odds with the more laidback approach of Rijkaard.

Maybe, in hindsight, Rijkaard provided Messi's finishing school. He had allowed the young man to grow as a player. Maybe even as a man. In later years, Messi would say: 'All the coaches I had at first left me things, but I think the most important thing in my career was Rijkaard … he trusted me.' Under the Dutchman, he had experienced incredible highs and quite a few lows. There was a feeling, though, that while the future of the club was uncertain, Messi's was not. The young man had now entered his twenties, but he still held that child-like enthusiasm for the game. That would never change.

RED CARDS

One of Messi's great attributes is his calm temperament. He rarely retaliates, despite the often illegal treatment he gets from opposing players. His first and only red card is infamous. Sent off after just forty seconds of his international debut for Argentina against Hungary. Here is how his red card record matches up against some of the sport's greatest players up to the end of 2016.

Lineker

Messi

Maradona

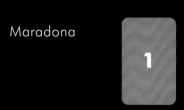

Maldini

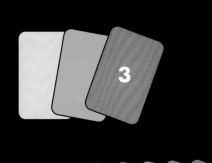

Gerrard

Beckham

C. Ronaldo

Pelé

Zidane

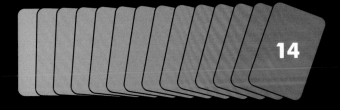

Ramos

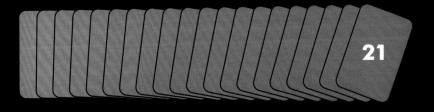

Growing as a player – in a sinking ship

A PEP TALK – AND FOOTBALLING GREATNESS AWAITS

4

'

PEP IMMEDIATELY TRANSMITTED AN ENORMOUS AMOUNT OF PRIDE IN OUR WORK, AMBITION AND HUNGER. HE WON OUR CONFIDENCE FROM THE FIRST DAY BECAUSE WE COULD SEE THAT THINGS WERE BEING DONE CORRECTLY AND THEN WHEN RESULTS STARTED TO FLOW THE CONFIDENCE GREW WITH THEM.

'

Lionel Messi, speaking in 2012

The statistics in these pages do some justice to the four years Lionel Messi spent under Pep Guardiola. It will tell you about their trophies – how they won everything in their first season together at Barcelona – and how Messi went from being one of the best players in the world to monopolising the Ballon d'Or award ceremony. There is also a lot to be gleaned from the stories about how there came to be such a synergy between coach and player. However, Guardiola's first two league games did not suggest the domination to come. In fact, Barça failed to win either game: they lost to Numancia and then drew at home with Racing Santander. But there was faith in his methods.

Sixteen years separate Guardiola and Messi in age, but in terms of footballing philosophy the pair could almost have been cloned. For the first part of his career, Messi had played with no real idea of his best position. Sometimes on the wing, mostly on the right side, with freedom to cut in. Guardiola adopted a front three of Messi, Thierry Henry and, despite his initial misgivings, Samuel Eto'o. The three players were all blessed with close control and pace – Eto'o the fastest of the trio – which could take them away from defenders when space was at a premium. Of the three, Eto'o was the most adept at closing down defenders in possession, but Messi's work-rate should not be ignored. Guardiola would later say: 'Messi wins the ball playing as the false number nine. If you put him at left-back, he would be just as good. He is the best defender in the world.'

Barcelona's relentless possession of the ball was given a name, tiki-taka, which came to symbolise dread for opposition teams, players and managers. The style pre-dated Guardiola but was synonymous with Spanish football and it's domination of the world and European game between 2008 and 2012. In terms of monopoly of the ball, Guardiola once said that you win it back 'thirty metres from [the opposition] goal, not eighty'. Frank Rijkaard and, before him, Johan Cruyff both used variations of the style at Barcelona, but Guardiola based his use on the playing resources available to him. His Barcelona side were all brilliant technicians, but what they clearly lacked was the physicality to bully sides. Messi, Andrés Iniesta and Xavi were the team's dominant personalities, but they were not likely to win many battles of strength, each standing less than five feet nine inches tall. Guardiola had also recently added the dynamic right-back Dani Alves, who was fast but slight. The centre-back positions were strengthened by the imposing Gerard Piqué, but his partner Carles Puyol was stocky rather than towering. The purpose of this brand of football was to dominate the ball and space and give opposition teams the feeling that they were being surrounded. When the other team had the ball, anyone in the Barcelona team had the licence to press that ball if it was in their zone, in the knowledge that when won back the ball could be recycled. They knew that every one of their teammates was comfortable in possession, including the goalkeeper. In Henry and Eto'o, the team had players who were always alive to the effects of this pressing game. Both could sweep in from left or right and score or create. What also became apparent was that Messi was adopting a different role. He could now play through the middle. With his natural zip and change of direction with the ball at his feet, it was no surprise he should be seen initially as an archetypal winger. But football was entering a phase when wingers had become passé. Wide men generally flourish when there is a centre-forward who can win duels and head the ball with accuracy and power. Barcelona had Henry and Eto'o, whose strengths were more than just their ability in the air. They were strikers who could scare and share. Messi was cut from a similar cloth, but he was limited in his ability to control and dictate games stuck out on the wing. The middle was where Messi should be and that is where he started to play. In that all-conquering season of 2008–09, Messi scored thirty-eight goals in all competitions. Eto'o scored thirty-six, Henry twenty-five. Many of those were made by the little man with magic in his boots. He was now becoming the conductor of the orchestra, but also the man who played the cello and the drums. He was certainly never idle.

The cast around Messi was changing as well. In addition to Alves and Piqué, the Barcelona squad included Alexander Hleb, a midfielder with dribbling and passing ability, Seydou Keita, who could fill a variety of positions, and a youngster promoted from the youth team called Sergio

Pep got closer to Messi than most
opposition defenders. They enjoyed
a close manager–player relationship –
often sharing their thoughts on matches
and how to approach the game.

Busquets, who generally operated in the space between defence and midfield. In some ways, Messi and Guardiola got lucky: all of a sudden there were players who fitted the profile of what was needed at the club. They allowed 'the Flea' to fly around organically. Busquets was not then, and is not now, an especially fashionable footballer, but he was a player who could screen while his more able colleagues went in search of goals.

The blip of those two opening games was soon forgotten as Barça put together a run of breathtaking brilliance. They won nineteen of their next twenty league games, and in three of them hit six goals. They were no less impressive in the Copa del Rey or the Champions League. Despite such a free-scoring year, Messi managed just one hat-trick. But he was still evolving into the goal machine he would become. He would still, from time to time, play on the right side of the field with the notion that his position was less important than what he was doing. But the 'false nine' role that some think was invented for him, became more frequent as the season went on. More importantly, Messi was now fit.

Perhaps, at this stage of his career, the most important member of his own squad was his personal nutritionist, Juanjo Brau, who tracked his movements wherever he went. There was no sense that Messi was not professional in his attitude towards the game, but in the quest to find out why he broke down so frequently, no stone was left unturned. His diet of red meat and plenty of carbohydrates was replaced by more fish and vegetables. He was advised to ditch the occasional late-night television, instead being prescribed more rest. Soon Messi was looking less like an overgrown teenager and more like the athlete he aspired to be. Though it does not sound like much, these simple changes to his habits and home life enabled him to play without fear of those niggling injuries reoccurring. In fact, the injury report card on him, which filled page after page in the early years, would be blank for the next three seasons. It was no coincidence that Barça racked up so many trophies during that period.

There was another side to this life-style change, and it was on the pitch. Like a number of young players, Messi was perpetual motion. His love of pressing the ball, and the man in possession, might have won him plenty of admirers and helped his team score lots of goals, but it came at a cost. This natural tendency meant he burnt energy at a frighteningly high rate, thereby leaving his body at a high risk of injury when he stopped and then started running quickly. Guardiola encouraged him to use his energy more sparingly, to stop feeling that he had to be at the hub of everything. He had to almost start to trust his teammates more to find him and engage his skills. Or as Johan Cruyff put it succinctly: 'When you play a match, it is statistically proven that players actually have the ball three minutes on average … So, the most important thing is: what do you do during those eighty-seven minutes when you do not have the ball. That is what determines whether you're a good player or not. You play football with your head, and your legs are there to help you.'

Cruyff, who coached at the club between 1988 and 1996, is considered to be the modern father of Barcelona. His influence as a player and then coach can never be underestimated. His teachings were absorbed by Guardiola, whose belief in them was transferred to his players with an eagerness along with the direct order for them to be adopted. The economy of movement that he preached would become essential to Messi's development. The lesson for Messi was clear: yes, he was a great footballer, with unique skills, but the next step in his development was to be a player who could dominate whole matches, even if he did not score. There would be games, against opposition who defended deep and with more intelligence, where his natural desire to dribble at high speed would be counter-productive. Better to keep the ball, to invite the opposition defenders to try and catch him in an area where the threat was less obvious. Or when, as Cruyff suggested, to play without the ball. To drift from zone to zone, without apparently playing any part in the game, before striking with either a killer run or pass. That economy of movement would lead to Messi having his best goalscoring season yet. It perplexed the experts: how can a man who appears to run so little have such an impact on games? It was just one of the many questions that the genius of Messi would provoke. As former Argentina coach Cesar Luis Menotti put it: 'Messi could be on the pitch talking to his wife and son on his mobile … then suddenly grab the ball and win the match.'

Messi's growth inspired Barcelona. The season 2008–09 saw them beat all-comers, and by some margin. In La Liga they blitzed teams. They finished with eighty-seven points, with just five defeats in their thirty-eight games and 105 goals scored. They led the table from week nine of the season. The highlights, as always, came in the big games and in particular against Real Madrid. In the middle of December they faced the then champions at Camp Nou. Real had sacked Bernd Schuster, the manager that led them to the title the previous season, and replaced him with Juande Ramos. Barcelona dominated the game but were only rewarded in the final ten minutes with goals from Eto'o and Messi. Real had mounted a defensive rearguard that was based on surrounding Messi, and if that did not work, just foul him instead. Royston Drenthe and Sergio Ramos were both booked for illegal defending against him. But the Catalans, despite feeling slightly frustrated, kept their patience, knowing that after conceding seventy per cent possession their opponents would have little left if and when the breakthrough came. After Eto'o scored the first, Messi was fed by Thierry Henry on a clear breakaway that started in the Barcelona half and ended when he chipped Iker Casillas. Occasionally disheartened, and certainly bruised and battered, Messi was proving even with the game won, he still had an eye for the main chance.

The second El Clásico that season was far more memorable. It had seemed when Real lost at Camp Nou that they were all but out of the running for the Primera División title. But a sequence of seventeen wins from eighteen games meant they were just four points behind the league leaders. They had a pretty decent team, too, with world stars such as Gonzalo Higuaín, Fabio Cannavaro and Raúl, not to mention fierce competitors in Casillas, Ramos and Gabriel Heinze. They even dared to take the lead through Higuaín. But a Messi-inspired Barcelona cut Real open at will. The little man was at the heart of the equaliser, advancing from the left wing and chipping the ball over for Thierry Henry to finish from twelve yards. After Carles Puyol added a second, it was Messi who profited from an interception by Xavi thirty yards out and ran in from the right, beating Casillas with the neatest of flicks from his left boot. In that goal, Messi showed why his range of gifts is so admired. With the majority of players, the debate it is not about how they are going to finish, but if they can at all. Twelve yards out and Messi has such an array of possibilities to end the move that it is sometimes hard to believe that he will choose the easiest. It was nonchalant, simple and exquisite. His second goal, and Barcelona's fifth, was again of immense quality and simplicity. He had the ball twenty-five yards from goal, almost set up for one of those dribbles that take him past tiring defenders who are begging to be put out of their misery. Instead he passed to Xavi and carried on running. With a swivel and turn, Xavi found him with a reverse pass. Messi emerged between Heinze and Cannavaro on the right edge of the area, his path unfettered. Casillas showed him the right side of the goal, as if to say he had his left covered. Messi feinted twice as if he was undecided on what to do and then drilled the ball to the left of Casillas. By the time he kicked the ball, he was maybe six yards from goal, ignoring the perceived wisdom of shooting as soon as the ball was under control. Even more remarkable was where Messi turned up during the game: his assist for the first goal was from the left wing, his first goal came from a central position and the last from the right. In all three positions he looked as if he had played there all his life. The Spanish paper *Sport* described Messi as 'Maradona, Cruyff and Best rolled into one'.

Despite these remarkable moments, Messi's finishing was still a work in progress. He had missed more than he scored that night, but then the mark of the true greats is how they respond when not everything goes their way. Later that week, he would find that other teams were formulating plans to cope with his genius. Barcelona had reached the semi-finals of the Champions League and been drawn against a formidable Chelsea side. The first leg at Camp Nou ended goalless. At Stamford Bridge in the return, Barcelona trailed after nine minutes through a stunning goal from Michael Essien. Messi was marked out of the game by a tenacious Chelsea, brilliantly drilled by the veteran Dutch coach Guus Hiddink. Barça had ridden their luck not to concede several penalties. They were down to ten men with seconds of

Maybe the greatest coach of his era; maybe the greatest player of any era.

A Pep talk – and footballing greatness awaits

injury time remaining when Messi picked up the ball on the left edge of the penalty area. Rather than attempt the type of dribble that had been thwarted all evening, he squared the ball to teammate Andrés Iniesta. The midfielder lashed the ball into the net for the equaliser that took Barça through to the final on the away-goals rule.

Next up was the first final of the season, the Copa del Rey, against Athletic Bilbao. Despite the Champions League and La Liga success of the mid-noughties, the Copa del Rey had eluded Barcelona for more than a decade. The wait looked like it might last longer when Bilbao's Gaizka Toquero scored within ten minutes on a fiery night at Valencia's Mestalla stadium. A stunning individual goal from Yaya Touré had Barcelona back on level terms before Messi took over in the second half. His goal, Barcelona's second, came after sharp work down the team's right led to a loose ball in the centre of a packed penalty area. Messi took control, evaded the outstretched legs of one defender before hitting a low shot into the net. Three minutes later he threaded a pass for the young Bojan Krkic to run through and score. In the end Barça won 4–1. Their league title was assured a few days later when Real Madrid, the only team who could catch them, were beaten.

When it came to Rome and the Champions League final, opponents Manchester United would have noted how Chelsea had blunted Messi and Barcelona in the previous round. Sir Alex Ferguson's United were a side of immense quality, having won the Premier League, as well as the League Cup and the Club World Cup. Their powerful attacking line-up included Wayne Rooney, Carlos Tevez and the world player of the year, Cristiano Ronaldo. With defenders of the quality of Rio Ferdinand, Nemanja Vidić and Patrice Evra, this was a United side who could mix it and also attack with sumptuous quality. The inclusion of midfield anchormen Michael Carrick, Anderson and Ryan Giggs made United a more complete team than earlier versions. Indeed, they threatened constantly during a frenetic opening ten minutes. After that, Barcelona took over with goals by Eto'o and a second-half header from Messi. The British press were not alive to the genius of the boy wonder until they had seen it with their own eyes. The idea that United could play more defensive midfielders, and that would stop the smallest man on the field, was a misreading of what Messi and Barcelona had become. The Spanish press, while lamenting the poor nature of United, paid special tribute to a player who belonged to another country, but had been adopted as one of their own. 'The Flea scores a goal with his head and demonstrates to Cristiano Ronaldo that he is the true king', said *El Pais*.

Messi enjoying a practice session on a cold and windy night in Stoke.

A Pep talk – and footballing greatness awaits

The summer of 2009 saw more changes at Barcelona. The most notable was the departure of Samuel Eto'o after five glorious years at Camp Nou. In his place came Zlatan Ibrahimović from Inter Milan for a fee in excess of €66 million (£57 million). Over in the Spanish capital, Real responded by embarking on a spending spree never seen before in world football. Kaka, Xabi Alonso and Karim Benzema all arrived, and so did Cristiano Ronaldo. He and Messi would, in time, be involved in the kind of scoring contest that would turn the record books upside down. Barcelona's big purchase provided a stylistic problem. Ibrahimòvić, for all his talents and skills, liked to play through the middle as an orthodox centre-forward with a range of unorthodox skills. Every team he played for before and since made him the main man. But Arrigo Sacchi, the man who made AC Milan great, retorted: 'Ibrahimović is a fantastic player. But he is too much of an individualist in what is a team game. I advised Pep Guardiola not to sign him.' Later, Ibrahimović would claim, with no real malice, that Messi's desire to play through the middle was what killed his chance of being a success at Camp Nou. The Swede also had well-documented issues with Guardiola. Indeed, in his autobiography he claimed to have hardly spoken to the Spaniard once he was dropped from the first team, and described him as a 'spineless coward'. His numbers that season were still pretty impressive, but they paled in comparison with the man who claimed the central role he craved. Messi featured in thirty-five Primera División games that year and scored thirty-four goals. There were other goals in other competitions as well. The emergence in 2008 of the lightning-quick Pedro meant that the absence of the blistering pace of Eto'o was not so keenly felt as feared, and it was Pedro who scored the winning goal in the final of the Club World Cup. Messi had scored earlier in the game, and when he stood to receive his medal he might have wondered when the success would end. It was the sixth medal he collected in 2009. Along with the league title, the Champions League, the Copa del Rey, there was also the Spanish Super Cup and the European Super Cup.

In an effort to retain the La Liga title, Barcelona would have to be a model of consistency, given the frightening power that Real Madrid now possessed. Barça were never out of the top two all season, pursued doggedly by Real, managed for that one season by Manuel Pellegrini. The league was decided by the meetings between the two sides, particularly the one at the Bernabéu in the second half of the campaign. The game was goalless after half an hour, with Messi on the end of some uncompromising defending. Whenever he was fouled, though, Messi's sheer love for the game prevented him from making any injury seem worse than it was. His immediate reaction was to find the ball and restart the game as quickly as possible. On this occasion, he squared the latest free-kick to Xavi, perhaps aware that for just a moment Real were keeping a higher line than necessary. He kept on running, anticipating a pass from his teammate. It came and suddenly he was free. The rest was not simple, the chipped pass needed to be controlled on his chest and that gave Real defender Raúl Albiol time to get back. But Messi fooled him by controlling the ball to his right and then striking the ball on the rise, giving Iker Casillas no chance.

It was a pressure-point match, yet Messi responded as if it was just another game. Real were top and a win for them could have ended the title race. Both sides were far and away the best in the Primera División that season, with Valencia trailing them by more than twenty points in third place. So if Barça had slipped up, they could not hope for help from any of the other teams in the league. But Barça took fate out of the equation, with a second-half goal from Pedro confirming a 2–0 victory. Their league form was nearly beyond reproach: one defeat all season, at Atletico Madrid, thirty-one victories, six draws and ninety-eight goals scored, more than a third of them by Messi.

Barcelona's attempt to defend all their titles failed, but there were still notable personal highlights for Messi. In the quarter-final of the Champions League, Barcelona drew Arsenal. In the first leg at the Emirates Stadium Messi had been overshadowed by Ibrahimović, who scored both goals in a 2–2 draw. In the second leg, Arsène Wenger's side took an early lead and Barcelona looked a little nervous. In terms of style, Arsenal's use of the ball, and their intricate passing and movement, most closely resemble Barça. But on this night in 2010, one man stood above all others.

219
APPEARANCES

80
ASSISTS

211
GOALS

14 TROPHIES

2008–09

2008–09

2008–09

2009

2009

2009

2009–10

2010

2010–11

2010–11

2011

2011

2011

2011–12

 Copa del Rey

 La Liga

 UEFA Champions League

 Spanish Super Cup

 FIFA Club World Cup

 UEFA Super Cup

A Pep talk – and footballing greatness awaits

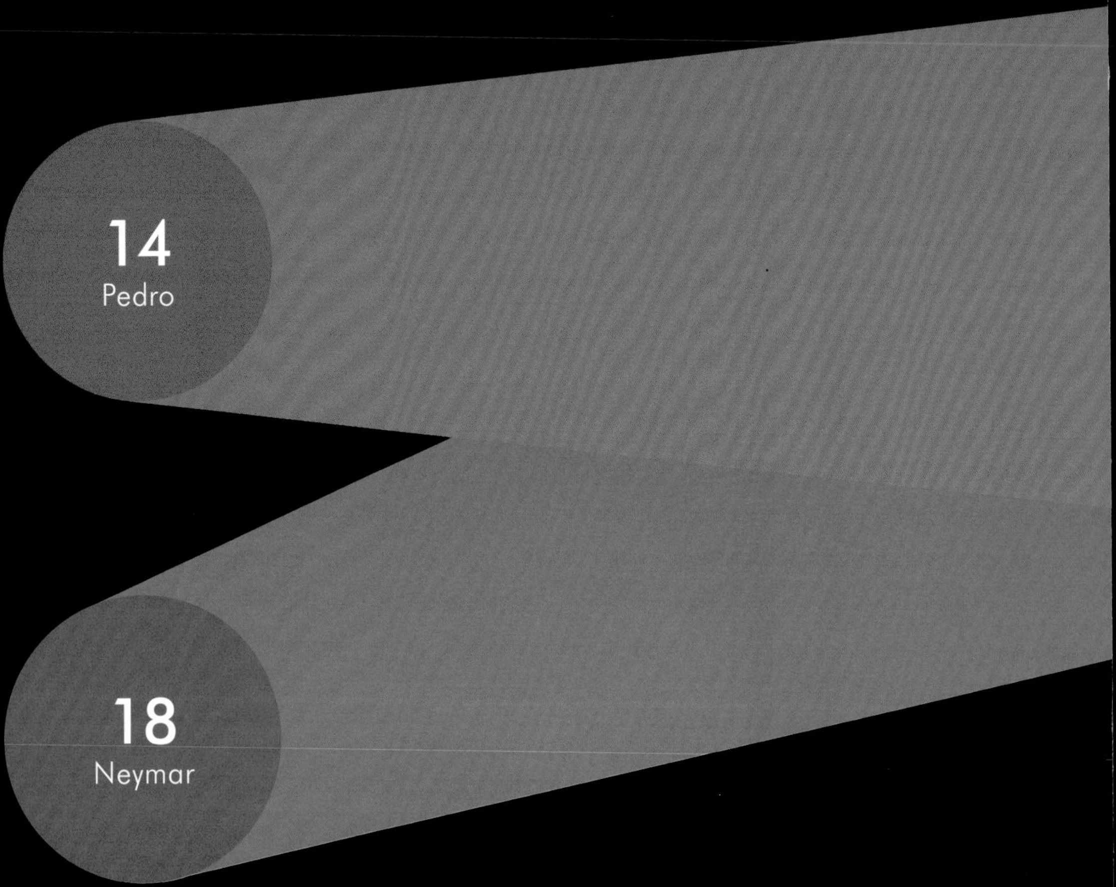

14
Pedro

18
Neymar

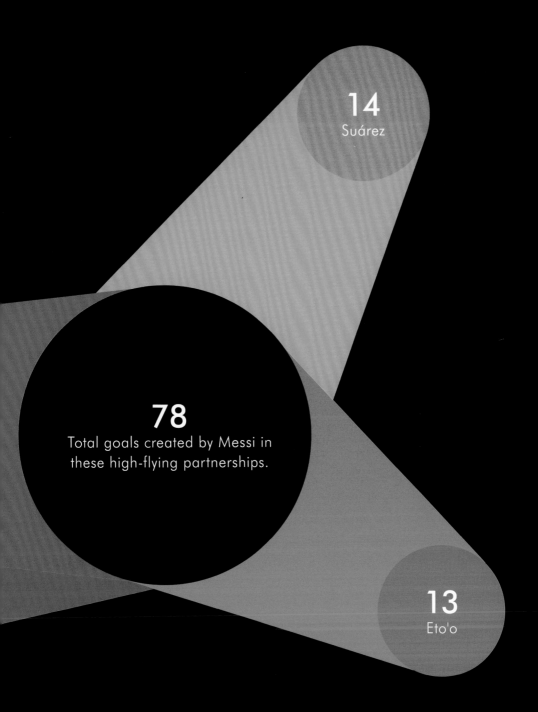

14
Suárez

78
Total goals created by Messi in
these high-flying partnerships.

13
Eto'o

Messi's first goal came from persistence. He dribbled from the right to the centre, his attempted pass to Xavi rebounded back into his path and a rasping left-footed shot left Manuel Almunia helpless. That sense of perpetual motion brought him a second sixteen minutes later. He started the move centrally, playing the left-back Éric Abidal into a threatening positon. When Abidal's cross was defended, there appeared little danger. But Pedro picked up the ball and fed Messi fifteen yards out. He took the ball past Gaël Clichy and dinked the ball with his right foot over Almunia. His third emphasised how many different kinds of finishes he has at his disposal. Played in from the halfway line, he ran on and then with the keeper doing what he could to narrow the angle, Messi chose the lob as his preferred option. Allowing the ball to slow, he got his left foot under the ball and lifted it into the net. 'The pictures do more than I can', said Sky commentator Andy Gray. The game may have been over to all intents and purposes, but Messi added a fourth in the second half, ghosting past Arsenal defenders and scoring at the second attempt. It left Wenger in awe. 'He is like a PlayStation player', he said. 'He can take advantage of every mistake you make. He can make a difference at any moment.'

However, even Messi can be given to outbreaks of fallibility at times as he showed in the semi-final against an Inter Milan side drilled to defensive perfection by José Mourinho. In particular, the Portuguese Manager asked his captain, the Argentine midfielder Javier Zanetti, to follow Messi wherever he went, whether it was central or on either wing. After taking the lead, Barça crumbled to a 3–1 defeat, with Messi marginalised. They fared little better in the second leg, scoring just one goal despite playing against ten men for much of the game. This time, Mourinho detailed Zanetti and Cristian Chivu to try and stop Messi. And they did. If Messi felt his footballing life was about to get harder, he received the worst news when Mourinho brought his brand of football pragmatism to the La Liga as Real Madrid manager.

The culmination of Messi's year came during the annual awards season. In 2009, there were two prizes that heralded the best player in the world. The Ballon d'Or was then an award given to the best player in European football as voted for by journalists appointed by the publication *France Football*. It had been won a year earlier by Cristiano Ronaldo. In 2009, 473 of the points available were in favour of Messi. The next highest was Ronaldo, who received 240 fewer points. The FIFA World Player of the Year award was similarly awarded to the Argentine. It would be the last time the awards were presented separately. Both organisations realised they were coming up with the same winner. After finishing second the year before, this honour underlined how important Messi's contribution had been in Barcelona winning the 'sextuple'. 'Honestly, I knew that I was among the favourites because Barcelona had a fruitful year in 2009', Messi told *France Football*. 'But I didn't expect to win with such a margin. The Ballon d'Or is very important to me. All the players who won it before were great players, and some great players never won it.'

The voting for the World Player of the Year was just as comprehensive, with Messi receiving 1,073 votes from the captains and coaches of the men's and women's national sides. Again, Ronaldo finished second, 721 votes behind. Included in the nominees for both awards were other Barça stars Xavi, Andrés Iniesta and Samuel Eto'o (now of Inter). But such comprehensive voting in favour of Messi by so many independent figures, was an indication of how he was now being perceived outside Catalonia.

WHO HELPS MESSI SCORE THE MOST?

Barcelona are renowned for their free-flowing, team-first style. These high-scoring assists showcase their talent for passing and creating, and especially highlight the important influence of Dani Alves in creating chances for Messi to find the net. Figures record assists in the La Liga up until the end of the 2015–16 season.

26
Dani Alves

18
Pedro

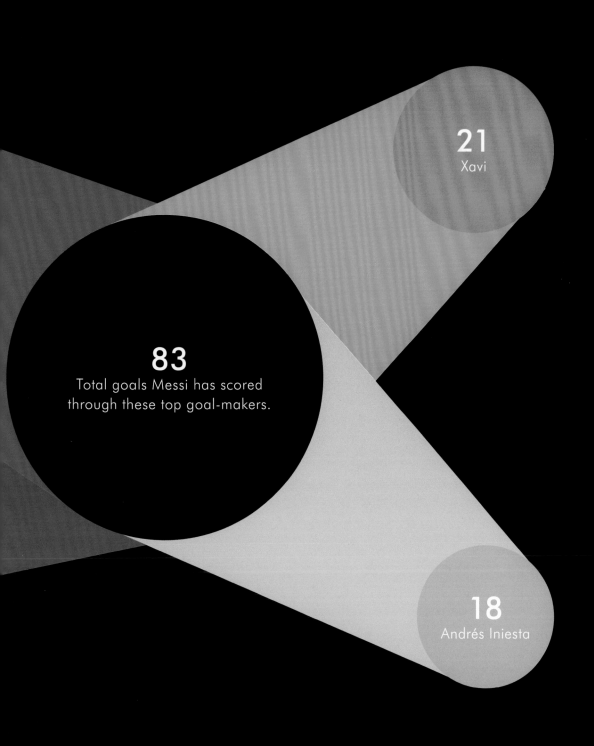

21
Xavi

83
Total goals Messi has scored
through these top goal-makers.

18
Andrés Iniesta

EL CLÁSICO – YES THOSE ONES

5

'
I WAS LUCKY THAT I PLAY[ED] WITH ZIDANE, WITH CRISTIANO RONALDO, WITH RONALDO, WITH FIGO...BUT AGAINST, I THINK MESSI... [HE] IS VERY DIFFERENT; HE MAKES EVERYTHING LOOK SO EASY, SO EFFORTLESS – EVEN IMPOSSIBLE.
,

Raul Gonzalez, Real Madrid's second highest ever scorer

There are derbies – and there are rivalries. Manchester United versus Manchester City is about local bragging rights. But Manchester United versus Liverpool is about history, bitterness and about the cities' status beyond the football pitch. Barcelona has a local rival in Espanyol, while Real Madrid shares the Spanish capital with Atlético. But Barça and Real measure their success by how they do against each other; into this maelstrom stepped the uncrowned king of conflict, José Mourinho. He arrived at the Bernabéu knowing he had arguably the best squad in the world and that he had demonstrated at Inter Milan how to stop Lionel Messi.

Barcelona and Messi had started the 2010–11 season in uncertain fashion. Messi had scored Barça's first league goal of the season, but a 2–0 defeat at home to Hércules made some wonder whether this was the end of the cycle at Barça. 'The third year,' the great Hungarian coach Béla Guttmann always said, 'is fatal. If a manager stays at a club more than that, his players tend to become bored and/ or complacent and opponents start to work out counter-strategies.' This was Pep Guardiola's third year at Barcelona and the third season in which Lionel Messi was being projected as their major star. They would

THE GOLDEN RATIO

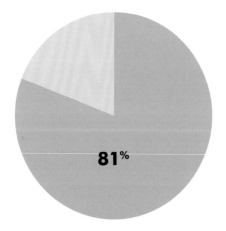

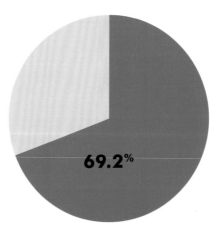

Career Goal Ratio
Messi averages a goal in 81% of all the games he plays in.

Overall win ratio
In just under 70% of all the games Messi plays in, he is on the winning side.

enter the first El Clásico of the season on the back of six consecutive league wins, culminating in a comprehensive 8–0 victory at Almería, three of the goals from Messi. Real Madrid came to the contest after seven consecutive wins, had yet to lose a game and were top of the Primera División. It seemed as if a changing of the guard was on the cards.

There were 98,255 people crammed into Camp Nou for a game played on a Monday. It turned out to be a truly manic Monday. The pace of the game was comparable to the fiercest derbies. Except that Real, with Cristiano Ronaldo at the peak of his powers, and an array of talent in other positions, chased shadows for most of the night. In the summer, Barcelona had let Zlatan Ibrahimović leave on loan and signed the prolific striker David Villa from Valencia. In Villa, Messi had a partner in attack who worked tirelessly and made the type of forward runs that Messi's perceptive passing could pick out. On this night, Messi not only scored, but his influence could be felt from the start. By the touchline, from an angle too acute for protractors, he curled in an early shot that beat Casillas but hit the woodwork. What was also noticeable was how Messi was instantly surrounded by Madrid players. Mourinho's

73.8% Win

15.8% Draw
10.4% Lose

Barcelona win ratio with Messi starting (Based on 2009–2015)

aim was to swamp the danger man. But Messi's movement was so adroit that he was still involved in the move that led to the first goal: passing to Iniesta inside the Real half, before he found Xavi, who had swapped with Messi to play the centre-forward role for this chance, to flick the ball past a despairing Iker Casillas. For the second Messi was involved in the same position, seemingly on the periphery of the game but bringing in players to decisive effect. A cross from Villa allowed Pedro to score after Barcelona had kept possession of the ball for nearly a minute.

The second half revealed how Messi had already built up an understanding with Villa. Messi spotted a weakness on the Madrid left, and when Dani Alves had the ball, Messi went to him, demanding it. He was maybe thirty yards from goal, but his dribbling from side to side made him elusive for the Real defenders. He waited for Villa to make his move before caressing the ball into his path for goal number three. It was the same combination for goal four. Messi picked up the ball in his own half and accelerated into opposition territory. He beat two players and spotted Villa making a run in the left half of the pitch. His head up, Messi drilled the ball low between Real defenders and the forward finished simply.

THE AVERAGE TACKLES MADE PER GAME

Messi's relatively high tackle rate during his Champions League career, especially given his position, shows his commitment to all areas of the game.

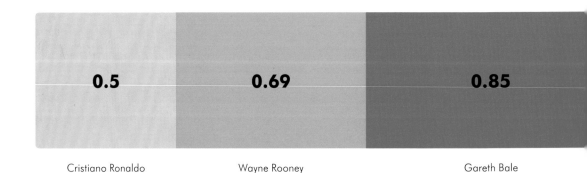

| 0.5 | 0.69 | 0.85 |
| Cristiano Ronaldo | Wayne Rooney | Gareth Bale |

The fifth goal was the only one that did not involve Messi. But he was still full of running, and late in the second half he was poised to dribble through the entire Real defence until Sergio Ramos intervened. The swipe at Messi's ankle earned Ramos another red card to the twenty-one he had amassed up to that point in his career. It was a foul born out of frustration; frustration that a game-plan designed to stop Messi had in fact allowed him to dictate the game. Ramos knew the battle had been lost, and the foul was probably the only meaningful contribution he made in this game. He was not helped by the players ahead of him, Xabi Alonso, Mesut Özil, Karim Benzema and Cristiano Ronaldo, who had not impacted the game. But Messi had: dropping deep, making passes, hitting the crossbar and creating goals.

The nightmare for Ramos was that there were four more El Clásicos to come that season. Indeed, Real and Barça would meet four times in seventeen days. The first was in the league at the Bernabéu on 16 April 2011, and had less intensity than might have been expected. Messi and Ronaldo swapped penalties in a 1–1 draw. The fact that honours were even was a moral win for the visitors: Barça led the league entering the game and Real's failure to get the win they needed meant there was no change at the top.

0.87   1.17

Lionel Messi   Ryan Giggs

The next chapter was four days later in the final of the Copa del Rey at the Mestalla Stadium in Valencia. It would be Real's only success against Barcelona that season with Ronaldo's extra-time goal ending their run of six meetings without a win. That the match was settled in extra time gave weight to the theory that, compared to Messi, Ronaldo was the fitter man, capable of superhuman feats even when others were fatigued. No one could argue that on the night, Real were superior. Barcelona seemed a team tired of always having to find a way of breaking down packed defences. Normally they would turn to their talisman to provide the spark. On this occasion, Messi did not deliver. But anyone with perspective could see this was the rarest of things for Leo: an off-night.

Messi would not have long to wait to prove he was very much at the peak of his powers because game three, a week later, was the first leg of the Champions League semi-final at the Bernabéu. Madrid's wait for *el décimo*, their tenth European Cup, had lasted longer than their fans anticipated. Number nine had been won in 2002, after all, but they had not been close since. It turned out to be a fractious night, filled with tension and animosity. Real were reduced to ten men when Pepe was sent off, Mourinho was sent to the stands for his protests, and would watch the second leg from the stands. But while chaos ensued around him, Messi, all five feet seven of him, stood tall and delivered two late goals to give Barça the advantage. The game, though, often resembled a boxing match where the participants hope to rack up points for the best reactions to punches that did not land. It also emphasised that although Messi's genius allowed him to do things with the ball that others could only dream about, it was his instincts and vision that made him the player of his generation. The fact that his two goals came in the last fifteen minutes of a match in which he had absorbed a number of fouls, demonstrated that stamina and conditioning were now part of his armoury. The first goal came after smart work down the right with Messi ghosting in at the near post with a striker's finish. There are those that think Leo rarely shows emotion on the pitch, but there he was, turning to the small band of

Catalans behind the goal, grabbing his shirt and acknowledging that a goal against the old enemy was worth a bit more.

The second seemed the sort of goal that he had been scoring for fun for years. Picking up the ball on the halfway line, Messi dribbled past five Madrid players, all of whom stood off in the hope that the attacker was as weary as they were. The right-foot finish past Casillas gave Barcelona a second away goal. It was a reminder that Messi remained a dangerous, dynamic presence near the end of games. Again, he showed that it was the big games in which he always seemed to deliver.

Two away goals from the first leg is considered a pretty insurmountable lead and so it proved in the second leg, six days later. It was a comparatively tame 1–1 draw, and when Pedro scored in the second half it meant *Los Blancos* needed three. Instead Real committed twenty-seven fouls in the hope of breaking Barcelona's rhythm. Messi played mostly on the fringes, but there was still the sight of him nicking the ball from Real high up the pitch, and perhaps running more than normal. He played with a selflessness that is overlooked because his brilliance with the ball demands so much of our attention. But his contribution in making sure the Catalans kept the ball from Real Madrid – they had sixty-five per cent of possession that night – meant Barcelona were through to another Champions League final.

It was becoming increasingly clear that the little man was always pumped up when he faced Barça's arch-rivals. There are few better ways to make yourself a club legend than scoring against the team your fans despise. When the dust had settled after these four titanic clashes in such a short time, Barca were heading to Wembley Stadium as well as yet another Spanish League title. They still had a fully fit and firing Messi who was about to demonstrate in London that his powers were just as mercurial as ever.

MORE THAN JUST A LEFT FOOT

Zlatan Ibrahimović once said he wondered how good Messi would be if he used his right foot. Well, as this illustration of Messi's Spanish League goals demonstrates, he actually does use it, as well as his head.

HEAD
21 GOALS

CHEST
1 GOAL

HAND
1 GOAL

RIGHT FOOT
72 GOALS

LEFT FOOT
405 GOALS

500
GOALS

632
GAMES

201
ASSISTS

64
PENALTIES

25
FREE KICKS

38
HAT-TRICKS

El Clásico – yes those ones

THE MAIN MAN VERSUS THE MAIN MAN

6

'

MESSI IS A TEAM PLAYER AND HIS INDIVIDUAL BRILLIANCE IS PART OF SOMETHING BIGGER. RONALDO'S CONTRIBUTION ON THE OTHER HAND IS MUCH MORE LIMITED. HIS ROLE AT REAL MADRID IS THAT OF SOMEONE WHO FEELS THE BEST WAY TO HELP THE TEAM IS BY SCORING GOALS. THAT IS THE DIFFERENCE BETWEEN THE TWO OF THEM. MESSI ALSO SCORES A LOT OF GOALS AND USES HIS INDIVIDUAL CLASS, BUT NEVER LOSES SIGHTS OF HIS TEAMMATES.

'

Johan Cruyff speaking in December 2015

They play for different teams, come from different countries on different continents, and once a year they sit next to each other to find out which of them is the best footballer in the world. It has been that way for nearly a decade. Is there animosity between them? Maybe more than they say publicly, but their rivalry is much more part of our imagination. When they play against each other, neither fouls the other; it is all about which one walks off the winner. Messi has the honour of winning most of their little battles, but no one forgets about Cristiano. Their duel for supremacy has taken modern football to new heights.

Lionel Messi and Cristiano Ronaldo are the greatest players of their generation. Both are loved, revered and, in certain places, reviled. Both divide opinion. Messi is better, his champions argue, because he is a team player and it is not all about him. The other side will then suggest Cristiano has made himself into what he is, working so hard off the pitch to hone his abundant array of skills. They are both capable of scoring goals from all angles. They have dominated games on the highest stages and been rewarded with Ballons d'Or to cement their places at the top of the tree. There are similarities off the field: both come from humble backgrounds and have had to work hard for their achievements.

Theirs is, in some ways, a strange kind of rivalry because they are not trying to beat the other, and never hurt each other with words. Rather, they seek confirmation that they are the best in the world. Neither is content to be told that he is among the best the world has seen for a very long time. In fact, the only kind of negativity between the pair is their voting in the World Footballer of the Year awards. Messi often votes for his Barça teammates and Ronaldo has even gone as far as voting for Mesut Özil rather than Messi.

As their careers have lengthened, both footballers have redefined the positions in which they play, or have even reinvented them. Originally positioned as wingers with more than a handful of tricks, they have both grown into the central forward position, the structure of their teams built to suit their many skills. Their goal tally per season compares more than favourably with the best strikers in Europe. Rarely are there

complaints from their teammates that too much of the team's general play revolves around them; the likes of Luis Suárez, Karim Benzema, Neymar and James Rodríguez recognise why the idea is always to get the ball to Messi or Ronaldo. That is the aura their goalscoring has brought them, but more than that, the aura their technique and natural skill demands.

It is this command of matches, the natural instinct to lead play that separates Ronaldo and Messi from other elite players and why managers build teams around them. This can be seen in the insight of Sir Alex Ferguson and Luis Enrique describing their charges. For instance, Sir Alex Ferguson said in 2015: 'Messi is a fantastic player, it's like he's wearing slippers when he controls the ball. But here, for me, is the difference. Messi is a Barcelona player ... but Ronaldo could play for Stockport County and score a hat-trick. He has everything. He can shoot with both feet, head the ball, he's as brave as a lion. And here's something else people overlook: during my time at Manchester

United I was lucky enough to have a lot of people who put in countless extra hours to get better. Gary Neville turned himself from an average footballer into a wonderful one because of his work ethic, as did David Beckham. But Ronaldo used to completely exhaust himself, and still does. He just wanted to be the best in the world.'

Ignoring the fact that neither Ronaldo nor Messi are likely to play for Stockport County and prove Sir Alex right or wrong, the Scot is speaking from a position of intense knowledge of one and an observer of the other. It was Ferguson who put Ronaldo front and centre when he signed him for Manchester United from Sporting Lisbon in 2003, and helped nurture his talent until 2009 when he joined Real. It was Ronaldo who propelled United to three consecutive Premier League titles and a Champions League crown. If Ferguson is biased toward Ronaldo, then he cannot be blamed. But he never got to train Messi.

Likewise, Messi's coach at Barcelona, Luis Enrique, says: 'Messi is the best in the world without any doubt and for me the history of football.' Again, he may be an expert on Messi, but Enrique has never coached Ronaldo, he has simply been the man who asked his players to try and stop the Portuguese player. Maybe we should demur to someone who has played against both. Bayern Munich's French midfielder Franck Ribéry, believes: 'Messi is class. There is him, and then there is the rest. What he does is extraordinary.'

Two former players, who both played in attacking wide roles, are split on who is superior. Steve McManaman was a gifted, forward-thinking midfielder who won the Champions League twice with Real Madrid. Now a pundit for BT Sport, he knows what it takes to flourish in Spain season after season. 'His (Messi) goal record for Barcelona and the fact he never gets injured and his ability to sustain his level since he started as a boy because of his physique – I think it's amazing. I think we are blessed to have him around because he plays the kind of football we want to see and scores the sort of goals that we want to see. He behaves himself the way professional footballers should do. When he wins he is gracious, when he loses he is gracious. There is never a bad word about anyone. He is an example to everyone. When you go

Messi   Ronaldo

Games

32   28

Goals

21 16

Assists

13 2

THE SPANISH GIANTS

The Spanish giants Real Madrid and Barcelona have historically had a fierce rivalry, and since the arrival of Cristiano Ronaldo at the capital's side, this has only grown in the play-off between arguably their two greatest players.

Messi
Ronaldo

Goals for club
Goals for club

373

364

Assists
Assists

142

99

Appearances
Appearances

370

348

Messi
La Liga: 5 / FIFA Club World Cup: 3 / Copa del Rey: 3 / Ballon d'Or: 5 /Spanish Super Cup: 4 /
UEFA Super Cup: 3 / UEFA Champions League: 2 / European Golden Shoe: 3

Ronaldo
La Liga: 1 / FIFA Club World Cup: 2 / Copa del Rey: 2 / Ballon d'Or: 4 /Spanish Super Cup: 1 /
UEFA Super Cup: 2 / UEFA Champions League: 2 / European Golden Shoe: 3

The main man versus the main man

through history, and you think of Di Stéfano, Cruyff, Maradona, there's always one that stands out. But we've got Messi and Ronaldo, and every single year they challenge each other and push each other forward. I've got no problem with people saying they are equally as good.'

Trevor Sinclair, a marauding winger off the right and left wings, who played in the Premier League at Queens Park Rangers, West Ham United and Manchester City, as well as for England at the 2002 World Cup, said: 'Lionel Messi – he's the most alien-like player on this planet. He seems to ignore all those stereotypes that we have about footballers that they have to be big and strong. I think they're both (Messi and Ronaldo) extraordinary players. As a football purist, it's Messi for me. I think Ronaldo is more about power and athleticism. Hard work also – he's worked really hard. I think the way the game is going, players are more like avatars. Messi is lighter – tree trunks for legs and slight upper bodies and I think that's the way the game is going.'

It will never be possible to discern whether Messi or Ronaldo could have reached the levels they have without the presence of the other. That challenge of another great forcing the game, teaching others and pushing the other to discover more of their own talents. What the comparisons show is the growth of both players, their ability to keep improving in the face of emerging talent, under new management and as their own bodies change and develop.

Perhaps the two legends should not be compared, simply relished for what they have achieved. Both players were born to be great and the fact they live and play in the same era has propelled them to an even higher plane. Perhaps the defining, and underestimated talent of Messi is that he controls the tempo of games, inspires his teammates to dominate and manages to be both playmaker and goalscorer. Though he has acceleration, he is nowhere near the quickest, but it is the speed of his footballing brain that allows him to appear faster, to move with the momentum of play. It is this that separates him from others, including Ronaldo. The likelihood is that, barring serious injury, Messi will retire having scored and created more goals than his nemesis. The next question should be, was he a better creator or scorer?

More adulation for Messi as Cristiano Ronaldo looks for the right facial expression.

Former UEFA President Michel Platini hands Messi the trophy of Best Men's Player in Europe at the end of the UEFA Champion's league group stage draw ceremony. Cristiano Ronaldo's and Messi's supreme talents have made for fierce competition for this highest of accolades in the last six years.

The main man versus the main man

FREE KICKS

Total: 6

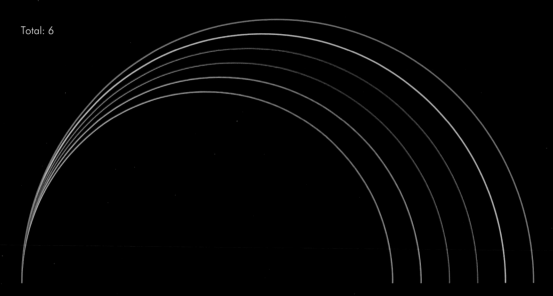

Zlatan Ibrahimović   PSG: 2 / Internazionale: 2 / Barcelona: 1 / Manchester United: 1

Total: 65

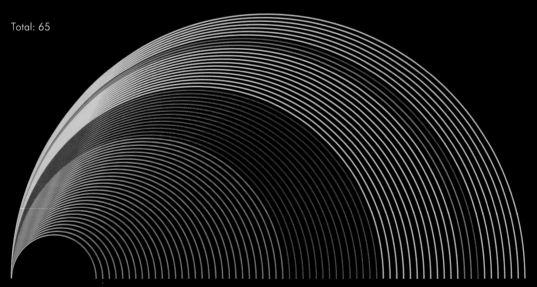

David Beckham   Manchester United: 29 / Real Madrid: 14 / LA Galaxy: 12 / England: 7 /
Preston North End: 2 / AC Milan: 1

Total: 28

Conversion Rate
8%

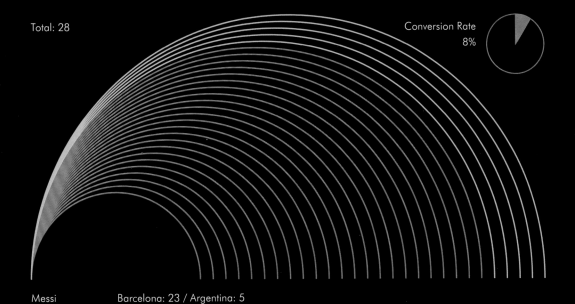

Messi   Barcelona: 23 / Argentina: 5

Total: 47

Conversion Rate
6.5%

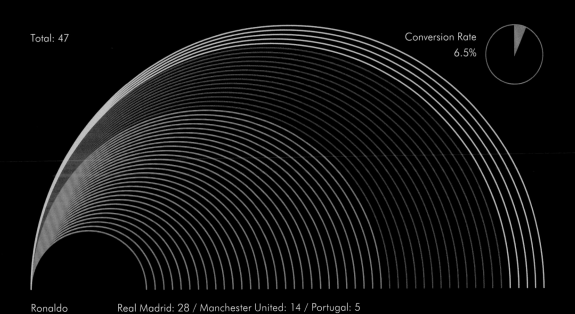

Ronaldo   Real Madrid: 28 / Manchester United: 14 / Portugal: 5

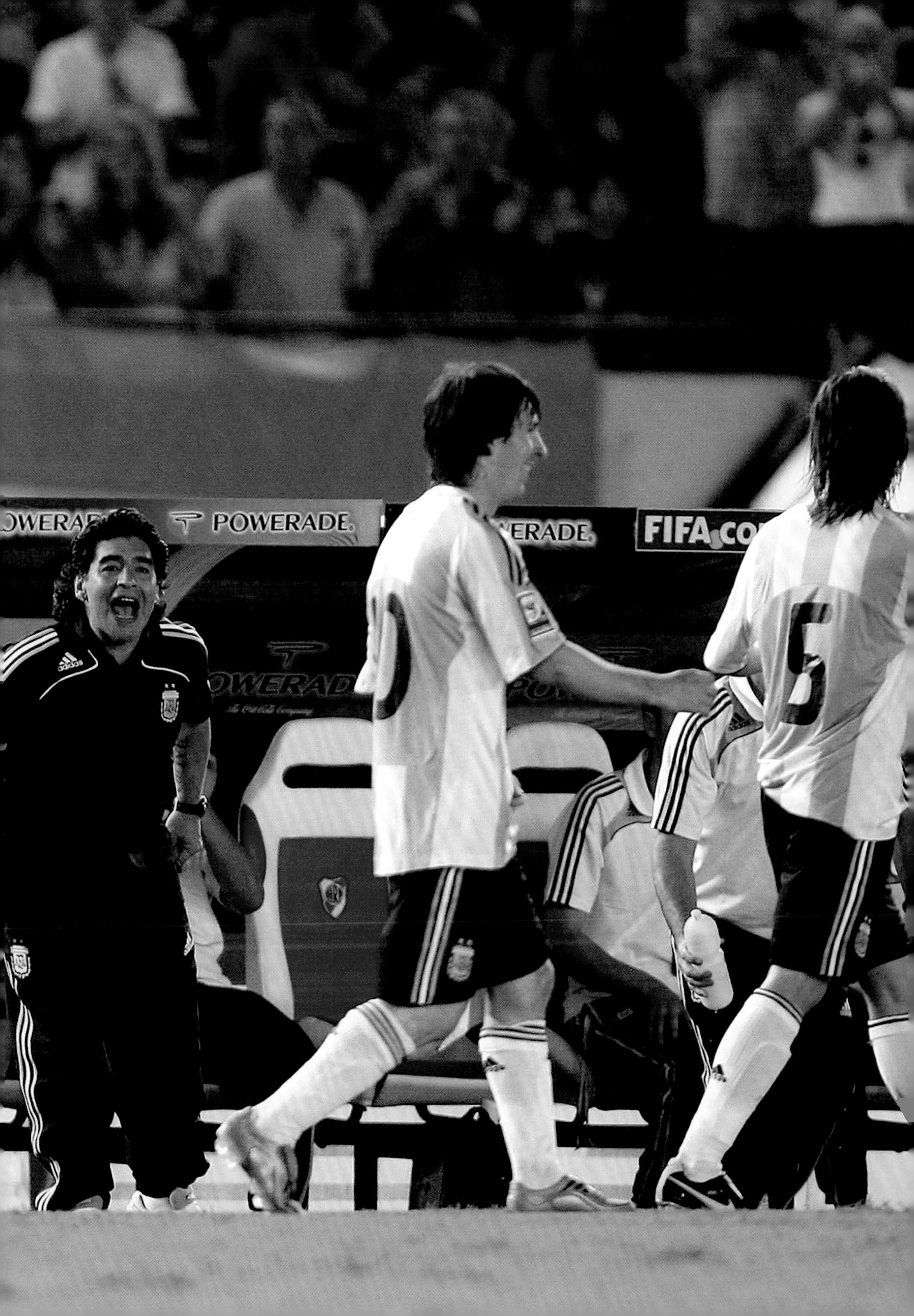
POWERADE.
POWERADE.
FIFA

LA ALBICELESTE – TALISMAN AND TORTURED

7

'

UNDERSTAND HIS SILENCES, BUILD YOUR TEAM AROUND HIM, GIVE HIM THE BALL, AND NEVER, NEVER, SUBSTITUTE HIM.

'

Pep Guardiola's advice to Argentina coach Alejandro Sabella about Messi in 2011

The date is 23 August 2008, the location the Bird's Nest Stadium in Beijing. Argentina have just beaten Nigeria in the football final at the Summer Olympics to win the gold medal. It was the first international glory the country had enjoyed since the Copa América of 1993. But the quality of this Argentina team, an under–23 set-up, suggested that something was changing. Angel Dí Maria scored the winning goal, but also in the side were Pablo Zabaleta, Javier Mascherano, Sergio Agüero, and the most fêted of them all, Lionel Messi. A high calibre team also featured Fernando Gago, Éver Banega and Ezequiel Lavezzi. They represented a golden generation of Argentine football, one that would be capable of challenging the best for another decade.

Fast forward to 26 June 2016. The venue has shifted to the MetLife Stadium in New Jersey for the final of the Copa América between Argentina and Chile. In the intervening eight years, Argentina have reached three major finals, including this one. Yet they have won nothing. They lost the World Cup final to Germany in 2014, and the previous Copa América final, again against Chile in 2015. In five of those eight years, they had Messi, who according to the annual awards ceremony, was the best player in the world. Over the years, Argentina had nurtured the likes of Gonzalo Higuaín, Carlos Tevez and Nicolás Otamendi; this was not a side that had regressed in terms of personnel. However, on this night in America, the one player you would bet your house on missed a crucial penalty in the shoot-out that decided the outcome. The destructive emotional force of such a miss propelled Messi into his decision to announce his retirement from the international game with immediate effect after Argentina had lost 4–2 on penalties after a goalless 120 minutes.

Messi's Argentina career is a story that started with an Olympic medal and finished in despair, disappointment and a dramatic exit. The decision to retire was quickly rescinded, and little more than two months later he was scoring Argentina's winner in a World Cup qualifier against Uruguay. Nevertheless, the question remains: where did it all go wrong for Messi at an international level? Why has the world's best player nothing tangible to show for more than one hundred caps and his place as the country's all-time leading scorer?

The story started badly: Messi was sent off on his international debut within two minutes of coming on as a substitute. He has not seen red in more than a decade of playing football since. The 2006 World Cup was largely a wash-out for him: he entered it off the back of an injury sustained playing for Barcelona, scored one of the six goals during Argentina's thrashing of Serbia, but rarely featured in a campaign that ground to a halt in a penalty shoot-out against Germany in the quarter-finals. There was widespread criticism of the national coach José Pékerman for using the talents of the nineteen-year-old so sparingly.

There has always been a feeling among some Argentines that Lionel Messi does not belong to them because he has spent the large portion of his career in Europe. Even though he often promises to finish his career at Newell's Old Boys, that proclamation is not enough. 'Messi is a Spaniard,' the Argentine football journalist Gabriel Anello wrote the night after Messi announced his retirement. 'Let him stay in Spain. Us Argentines don't want him and don't need him.' His is an unusual case: of the eleven players who started that Copa América final in New Jersey, only Gabriel Mercado played his football in Argentina. The other ten were all based in Europe. However, with the exception of Messi, they all started their professional careers in Argentina. None of them, though, has faced questions about whether they care more for their club than their country.

Despite the disappointments of the 2006 World Cup and the 2007 Copa América final, when Argentina lost 3–0 to Brazil, Messi's international future was still a bright one. He had only just turned twenty and his potential was enormous. But whereas at Barcelona, the arrival of Pep Guardiola was about to bring a serenity and security to the club, the absolute opposite was true of Argentina. In December 2008, Diego Maradona became the national coach.

To describe it as a strange decision would be an understatement. Whatever genius Maradona had as a player had not been transferred into his subsequent personal or professional life. Eccentric would be a mild term to explain the sense of chaos that surrounded the modern version of the legend; so would unreliable. Having been very ill during the early years of the twenty-first century, and having failed as a coach on two previous attempts in the mid-1990s, this was not a man who, either at the time or in hindsight, was stable or measured enough to lead Argentina. But for the romantics, a different picture was being painted. Maradona had once anointed Messi as his successor, heaping praise on the young man's shoulders when he started to make a name for himself. Maybe what Messi needed to perform superhuman feats for country as well as club was a paternal figure, someone to take the pressure off him. Instead, it was Messi and his teammates, in particular Javier Mascherano, who became the leaders of that team rather than the manager. In fact, Maradona was once moved to say that the Argentina side was 'Mascherano and ten others', although that quote was made after he stopped managing them.

That things were going horribly wrong under Maradona became clear when Argentina found themselves in a desperate position in their 2010 World Cup qualifying campaign. With two games remaining, Argentina needed to win both to make it to South Africa. They had just suffered a 6–1 defeat by Bolivia on 1 April 2009, the heaviest loss inflicted on the two-time world champions. 'The likes of Messi, Javier Mascherano, and [Carlos] Tevez had no influence on the match whatsoever', wrote Goal.com. There were external factors: the match was played at high altitude and on an incredibly poor pitch. But Argentina's preparations were almost non-existent, highlighted by the fact they flew into Bolivia just two hours before kick-off. No one escaped the criticism that followed, not even Messi, who at that stage was on the verge of winning the 'sextuple' with Barcelona. Messi should have been dominating games with Juan Román Riquelme, but the fulcrum of Argentina's attack was absent after falling out with Maradona. The conditions in La Paz affected Messi greatly: he vomited after the game. The player offered no excuses for the defeat, but there were those already looking to the coach for reasons why Argentina looked such a mess. Messi kept with the party line that everything was all right behind the scenes. 'We have to get together and go forward because Argentina can't stay out of the World Cup', he said. 'The relationship with Diego is great. There are no fights.' But his evidence was not borne out by the statistics:

Diego Maradona, the man every Argentine footballer is compared to – even Messi.

Messi takes on two defenders during Argentina's World Cup qualifier against Bolivia, 1 April 2009.

La Albiceleste – talisman and tortured

Messi was averaging a goal every four games for his country, well below the one-in-two ratio he was maintaining at Barcelona.

Argentina won their final two qualifying games to make it to South Africa. But Maradona's continual fights with the media and the authorities, including the Argentine FA, meant the cracks were only being papered over. Argentina won their three group games at the World Cup against Nigeria, South Korea and Greece. Victory over Mexico in their last-16 match set up a game with Germany. Up until that point, Messi had been the orchestrator of some wonderfully flowing football. Argentina had scored ten goals in four games. The problem, however, was that Maradona's attitude towards defence left them vulnerable to the first team who attacked and defended in equal measure. A goal in the third minute from Thomas Müller showed how porous Argentina's back-line was. Things did not improve and they were crushed 4–0.

There were two schools of thought about why Argentina and Messi had not yet scaled the heights expected. The first was that wearing the blue and white did not appeal to him in the same way as wearing blue and red. That was plainly nonsensical. Messi tended to run more and in different areas when he represented his country, chasing the ball and starting more attacks than he did for his club. The more prescient opinion was that few international coaches understood how to get the most out of him. In the four years since Messi had played in his first World Cup in 2006, he had evolved as a player, and so had Barcelona as a team. The importance of the midfield trio of Busquets, Xavi and Iniesta should never be underestimated. It was their rhythm and control that helped Messi flourish. Pep Guardiola recognised when he came in that to get the best of Messi, and Barcelona, he needed only a few system tweaks. For the same to happen in Argentina's favour, it should have been obvious that they needed to play a brand of football akin to that seen at Camp Nou. Besides, the style of football Spain had played in winning the European Championship in 2008 and the World Cup in 2010 had the world enthralled. To entrust Argentina's campaign in South Africa to Diego Maradona, a coach with no formal training and whose principal skill seemed to be to motivate through being a legendary player, seemed a wasted opportunity. Not that Messi did not try to free himself of this apparent non-management: no player attempted more than his thirty shots at the tournament. He hit the crossbar twice and was inconsolable at the final whistle when Argentina suffered their drubbing at the hands of Germany. Naturally quiet at the best of times, Messi certainly knows not to speak out of turn about Maradona, especially when his fellow countrymen are listening. Maradona's popularity among Argentines is established, whatever the right and wrongs of his post-playing career conduct; he remains their hero. Of Messi, there is admiration and pride at some of his exploits, but he cannot come close to being held in the same affection as Maradona.

The Maradona era as a manager was short-lived. By the end of July 2010, he was no longer coach of Argentina. In his place came Sergio Batista, a coach with a track record of management in South America, but with no experience of managing on the international stage. His first task was to achieve what a string of Argentina coaches had yet not managed: get the best out of Messi. Batista had his own view about where Messi should play after a 1–1 draw against Bolivia at the Copa América of 2011. 'I was seeing Lionel the wrong side of the halfway line, and that cannot happen. He has to play in the last quarter of the pitch, there cannot be midfielders ahead of Messi.' Yet Batista's theory before the tournament had been to blend traditional Argentine muscle with the Barcelona style. Messi would play in front of a midfield shield comprising Javier Mascherano, Éver Banega and Esteban Cambiasso. Messi would then play in a mouth-watering forward three with two of Ezequiel Lavezzi, Carlos Tevez and Sergio Agüero.

Historically, Argentina have always enjoyed an abundance of striking talent. But Messi needed a special chemistry with the strikers around him. Messi always scored and created when playing alongside Samuel Eto'o or Zlatan Ibrahimović, but his more prolific days came when he was part of a more fluid front three, when he could move left, right or centrally. Strikers like Eto'o and Ibrahimović tended to hold their positions, but Messi flourished alongside David Villa and Pedro, two players more flexible in their movement. Of the three Argentine strikers, all had a tendency to drop deep, meaning they would occupy

PENALTIES SCORED AND MISSED

Figures correct up until the end of 2016.

20
Missed

71
Scored

the space that Messi favoured. It was why Batista believed he was too deep, because everyone else was. The midfield was the other problem: three defensive midfielders, all with merits, but who were more comfortable being destroyers, not fulcrums or enablers. This was not total football, it was compartmentalised football.

This lack of joined-up thinking pointed to the problems that afflicted Argentina during the Copa América of 2011. The tournament took place in Argentina, in front of fans expecting the team to add to their haul of two Copa América titles. Argentina played just four games in this tournament, and were never beaten in normal time, yet failed to get past the quarter-final stage, where they lost on penalties to eventual winners Uruguay. They scored just five goals to completely underwhelm the Argentine public. Not surprisingly, much criticism fell at the feet of Messi, who failed to register a goal. However, he received some unlikely sympathy from his former coach. Diego Maradona told the sports newspaper Olé that the Argentines were quick to say Messi 'was the best of all times; but if Argentina cannot win two games it has to be his fault. We are being unfair with Messi. The Argentines cannot treat the best player in the world like that.'

In the end, Batista was fired for Argentina's failure to find their way past the last eight. But everything about the 2011 version of Argentina spelled confusion. For Barcelona, Messi had just scored forty-seven goals in the season, helping them to a La Liga and Champions League double. Conversely, by this stage of his career, Messi had been playing for Argentina for six years, and had scored seventeen goals, only seven of them in matches that were not friendlies. Still no coach had found the solution to why he was struggling for the national team. The next man to try was Alejandro Sabella, a man with a record of coaching as an assistant at the highest level, and who had recently enjoyed significant success with Estudiantes. The first thing he had to sort out was Messi's future as an international player: the abuse he had received in the wake of Argentina's Copa América debacle was so personal that he wondered whether, at the age of twenty-three, he needed the aggravation. Much of the abuse centred on the perception that he was more Spanish than Argentine. But those who know him best say the life he led in Barcelona had influences drawn from the streets of his native land. Nothing would give him greater pleasure than to win something with his national team. Premature retirement was out of the question.

World Cup Final 2014. No one remembers
who came second – unless it's Messi.

The first thing he had to do, though, was address his slightly underwhelming goal tally when on international duty. Under Sabella, there was a change. From the disastrous Copa América campaign through to the eve of the World Cup in 2014, he scored twenty-one goals for Argentina. Seven of them came in qualifying games. Now he was also captain of the side, having taken over the armband from Mascherano. Included in that haul of goals were his first international hat-tricks, both coming in friendlies against Switzerland and Brazil. His third goal against Brazil was pretty spectacular, too. His first two goals had put Argentina into the lead, but Brazil had scored three of their own that night, and the scores were level going into the final six minutes. Picking the ball up on the halfway line, hugging the right side of the pitch, Messi began to run, the ball seemingly tied to his boot. The Brazil defenders, maybe struggling with fatigue on a warm night in New Jersey, sat off him as he moved infield. Indeed, Messi had not been challenged by the time he reached the edge of the Brazil penalty area. Even so, there appeared to be little danger until Messi spotted that the whole of the left side of the goal was exposed. He would need to curl the ball while dribbling at top speed. And he did. Sabella said: 'Messi is an extraordinary player and he has been for a long time. In the national team his recent performances have been good...'

The rejuvenation of both Argentina and Messi gathered momentum. Argentina qualified for the World Cup in Brazil with little trouble and were installed among the favourites for the tournament alongside Germany and Spain, the defending champions. Apart from Messi, Argentina now had an array of world stars, including Higuaín, Mascherano, Dí Maria and Martin Demichellis. Occasionally Sabella would go for a more pragmatic three-man defence and at others would see the options available to him and play the attacking football that suited his personnel. Their route to the final was aided by a straightforward three wins in three games at the group stages. The captain scored in each game, including a spectacular injury-time winner against Iran. Argentina scored six goals in their games, though they had conceded three, but had done enough to suggest the tag of favourites was merited.

WORLD CUP GOALS

Miroslav Klose (Germany) 16

Ronaldo (Brazil) 15

Gerd Müller (West Germany) 14

Just Fontaine (France) 13

Pelé (Brazil) 12

Lionel Messi (Argentina) 05

La Albiceleste – talisman and tortured

WORLD CUP ASSISTS

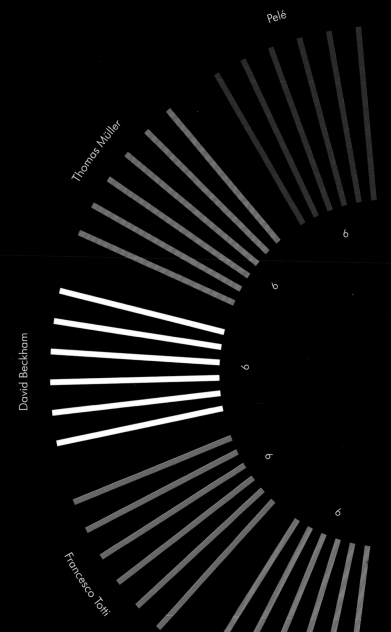

- Argentina
- Brazil
- England
- Germany
- Italy
- Poland

Pelé

Thomas Müller

David Beckham

Francesco Totti

Bastian Schweinsteiger

6

6

6

6

6

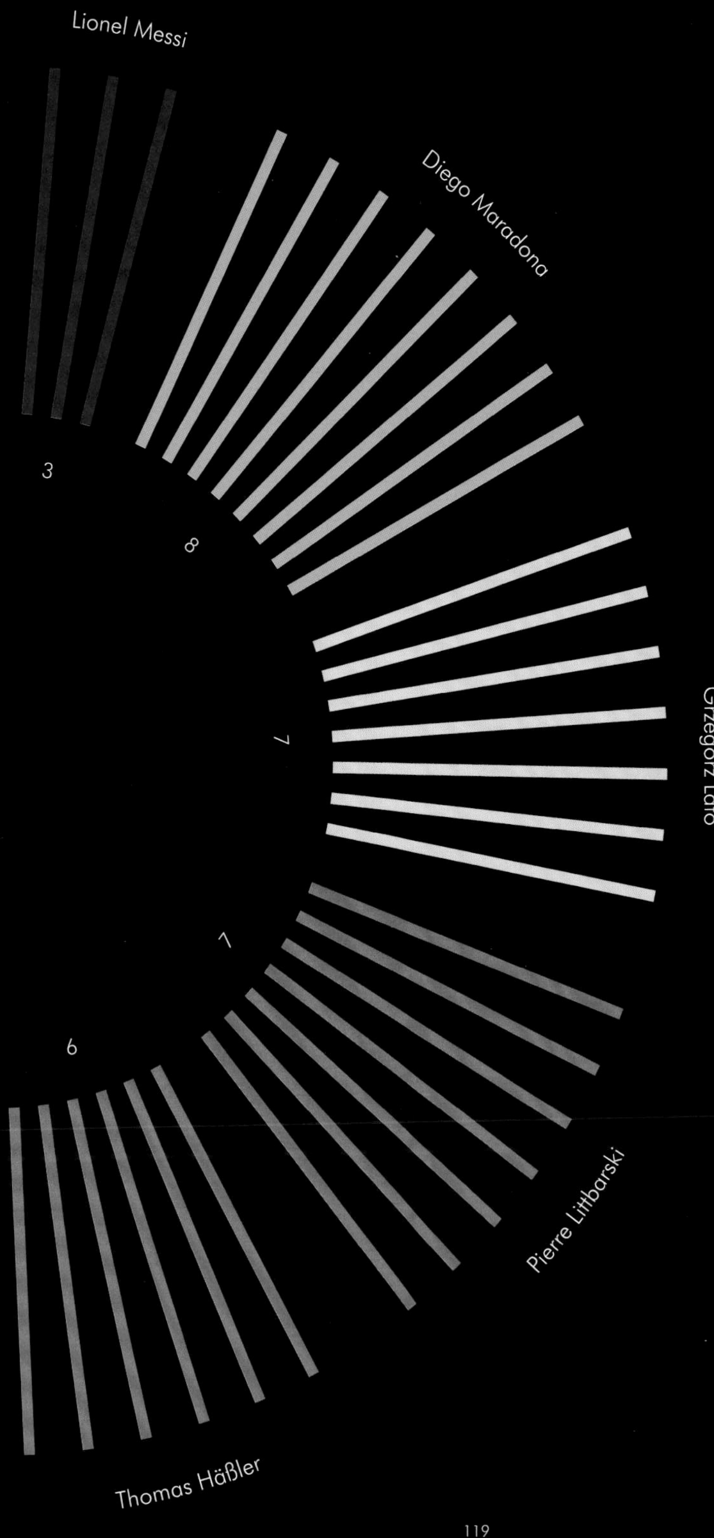

Lionel Messi

Diego Maradona

Grzegorz Lato

Pierre Littbarski

Thomas Häßler

3

8

7

7

6

La Albiceleste – talisman and tortured

Those results were soon forgotten when they entered the knockout rounds, and their first two games ended in 1–0 wins. Switzerland were beaten thanks to an injury-time goal from Dí Maria, fashioned from a typical slalom run from Messi. Belgium were then knocked out with an early strike from Higuaín. It set up a nervy semi-final against Holland settled via a penalty shoot-out after a goalless draw. The match is remembered not for another Messi masterclass, but a last-ditch challenge from Mascherano to deny Arjen Robben in extra time. No matter, Argentina had the showpiece they craved, and after Germany annihilated Brazil in the other semi-final, Messi was spared the ordeal of playing the host nation in the final. On 13 July 2014, Lionel Messi was going to take his place alongside the football gods, such as Pelé and Maradona, and crown his position as the best player in the world.

World Cup final
13 July 2014
Germany 1–0 Argentina
Maracanã Stadium

One hundred and seventy goals had already been scored during the tournament. Germany had accounted for seven of them in their previous match against Brazil. But both Argentina and Germany began the final in cagey fashion, perhaps too aware of how they could be hurt if they did not pay attention to the geniuses. Messi's moment, though, came in the first half. Running from the halfway line, left of centre, the ball at his feet, with only Manuel Neuer to beat. Only Manuel Neuer. The best goalkeeper of his generation. Whether it was the size of Neuer, or the significance of the moment, but Messi's shot drifted narrowly past the post. His chance had come and gone. Perhaps as a consequence, Messi vomited at half-time.

The tension heightened. Germany had graced finals of World Cups and European Championships for the past eighteen years without glory. But they had been building towards a triumph, their desire

Messi still dreams of the ultimate prize for his nation. His disappointment
clearly and strongly felt on the night Argentina came so close in their 1–0
defeat against Germany in the 2014 World Cup final.

La Albiceleste – talisman and tortured

tempered by the knowledge that another defeat could wound them irrevocably. Neither side dominated in the way they could. Germany had two-thirds of the possession, but were unable to translate that into tangible reward until the second period of extra time when Mario Götze grabbed the decisive goal. Germany held on to win the cup, and Messi's night was encapsulated by a free-kick that missed the target in the closing stages.

Messi's only award of the tournament was being voted its best player. There was much derision at the announcement, made as Germany ascended the stairs to pick up the trophy. How could a man who had played on the losing side, and who was not the top scorer in the tournament, win such a prestigious award? The criticism would almost certainly have passed the little man by; he was cocooned in his own personal torment. He may have been the world's best player, but he was still without a medal for his country. His walk to the dais showed all the pain he obviously felt.

Football at the top level is great when you win and desolate when you lose. Mario Kempes, the Argentine who did so much to help the country win the World Cup in 1978, said: 'Messi was not up to the challenge … I expect more from him.' Messi, though, is not the sort of player to answer his critics, firing back with his own criticism at a press conference. He may burn inside, but his nature is to retreat to his inner sanctum, digesting the criticism and then trying to answer the naysayers with deeds on the pitch. But the first chance he would get to do that was with Barcelona. International redemption was a way off and when it did arrive, there was more disappointment lying in wait.

After the World Cup, another coach was employed in the quest to make Argentina and Messi winners. Gerardo Martino was quickly becoming Messi's shadow, having coached Barcelona for a year. He went by the nickname 'Tata' and had much in common with Leo. He had played for Messi's childhood club Newell's Old Boys and had also managed them. He also came from Rosario. There is a video out there of a very small Messi doing tricks with the ball at Martino's testimonial. In one of his rare interviews, Messi had expressed his admiration for the brand of football that Martino had produced at the clubs he had served. There were claims that Messi received favourable treatment from Martino because of the coach's close relationship with Jorge Messi, but that was something Messi Junior denied.

A year after the World Cup, Argentina reached another final, at the Copa América in Chile. Again, there was further agony as the host nation took the trophy via a penalty shoot-out in which Messi was the only Argentine to hit the target. Twelve months later, in 2016, in a special Copa designed to celebrate the tournament's centenary, Argentina again reached the final. Again, the opponents were Chile. The result was once again decided by penalties. This time Messi missed his. And then came the words.

At the moment he announced his retirement from international football, Messi was the country's top scorer, with fifty-five goals in 113 appearances, overtaking Gabriel Batistuta during his final tournament. Very few of those fifty-five goals were just tap-ins. He also assisted in more than thirty goals for others, and hung up his boots after his best international tournament, in which his five goals included a hat-trick. However, the statistics also show that he never scored in any of the four finals he played. Neither, though, has Cristiano Ronaldo. But he has won one of his two finals.

Messi's retirement did not see out the summer. On 12 August 2016, he was saying: 'My love for the country and the shirt is too great.' Pressure had come from almost every corner. Not that the issues at the heart of Argentine football had been resolved to everyone's satisfaction. But perhaps Messi realised during that month of self-enforced exile how much he meant to the cause, that he was needed and loved.

After beating Colombia on the 15 November 2016, shedding the tag of the quiet one forever, Messi, in front of his Argentina teammates spoke for over a minute about why he and his colleagues were going to boycott the national media. 'We're very sorry it has to be like this but we have no option', Messi explained in the wake of accusations that teammate Ezequiel Lavezzi smoked marijuana after training. If anyone doubted whether the flea could lead from the front …

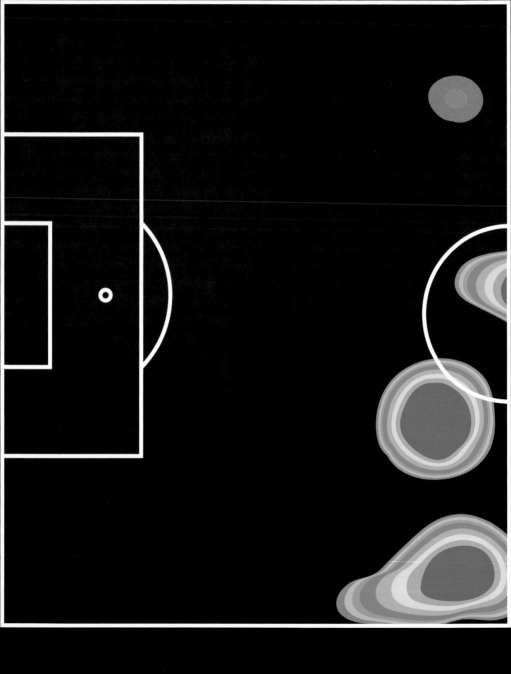

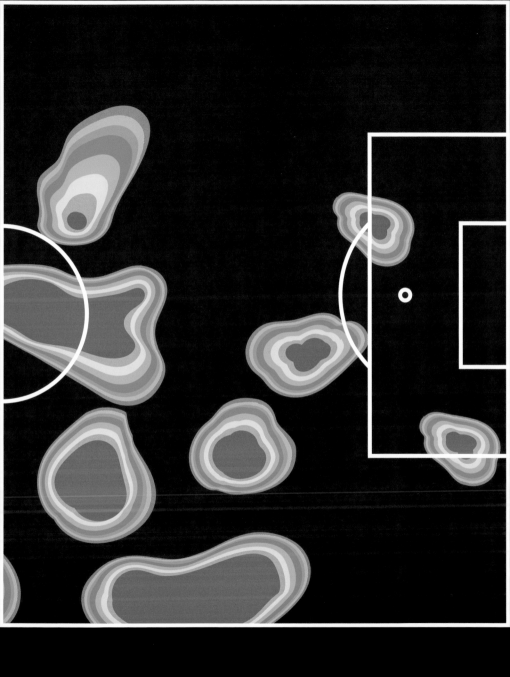

RELAX AND REBIRTH

8

'

IT WAS A CHALLENGE TO CHANGE THE IMAGE THAT I HAD GIVEN OUT LAST SEASON AND TO BE THE PLAYER I HAD BEEN IN PREVIOUS SEASONS AGAIN.

'

Lionel Messi, 2014

The boxer Mike Tyson was considered unbeatable in the late 1980s, having formed a perfect union with the training regimes of the Cus D'Amato and then one of his disciples, Kevin Rooney. When Tyson ditched the men who had been with him since the start, the cloak of invincibility slipped. Some may argue that his turbulent private life contributed far more to his downfall, but Tyson was never the same rhythmic brawler who destroyed lesser fighters. Similarly, Tiger Woods took domination of golf to a new level when Butch Harmon was his coach. At one point he held all four majors. But once the pair parted, Woods never quite reached those heights again.

Lionel Messi and Pep Guardiola may one day see each other and think: 'We had it pretty good.' The pair worked together for four years and won fourteen major honours. At times they were almost unbeatable. The extent of Guardiola's part in Barcelona's ascension during that time is open to debate. What the Spaniard did was help to make something beautiful after realising the prettiest girl in town had already been cast in his film. But after three years of making great sequels, the final episode did not have the happiest of endings. The 2011–12 Primera División title, which had been the preserve of Barcelona, went to Real Madrid. Barça's ninety-one points were dwarfed by the one hundred amassed by Real, who went to the top well before Christmas and never let go. Then in the Champions League, Chelsea attained some form of revenge for 2009 by holding Barça to a 2–2 draw at Camp Nou, despite playing with ten men for much of the game. Chelsea went on to win the title, beating Bayern Munich in a penalty shoot-out. Aside from the Spanish Super Cup and Club World Cup, Barcelona's biggest reward that season was winning the Copa del Rey, Messi scoring one of the three goals that comfortably beat Athletic Bilbao.

Despite the disappointing conclusion to the season, Messi's personal statistics were frightening. While Cristiano Ronaldo scored sixty in Real's title-winning campaign, Messi scored seventy-three. Of that tally, three came from free-kicks and fourteen from the penalty spot. The rest were from open play. He scored ten hat-tricks for his club and another two for Argentina. Perhaps the most famous of his trebles was the one against Bayer Leverkusen in the Champions League, when he became the first man to score five goals in a match in the competition. During a season when he played sixty games, and never suffered a serious injury, he also assisted in twenty-nine goals. There was no doubt he was becoming the most complete player in Spain, and arguably the world.

One of Messi's less well-known attributes is his capacity to learn and absorb from his teachers. Guardiola and Messi shared an incredibly close manager–player relationship to the extent that late one night, before an *El Cláscio*, Pep called Messi to explain a tactical innovation. 'Tomorrow in Madrid', he instructed, 'I want you to start on the wing as usual, but the minute I give you a sign I want you to move away from the midfielders and into the space I just showed you. The minute Xavi or Andrés Iniesta break between the lines and give you the ball I want you to head straight for Casillas's goal.' That conversation is credited with heralding the birth of the false nine position. However, not even Guardiola could have foreseen how well his player would take to it. The football writer Sid Lowe said that people did not realise that Messi adapted to any position on the field so well that 'he could be the best left-back or central midfielder if he was told to play there'.

Guardiola said something similar when trying to downplay his influence on the player. 'If he does what he does in the area, what do I have to do with that?' said the Spaniard after he had left Camp Nou for a year-long sabbatical before joining Bayern Munich. Guardiola said most of his knowledge of the player was based on conversations he had with his assistant, the late Tito Vilanova, the man who stepped into the manager's chair after Pep's departure. Vilanova would not oversee a full season at Camp Nou because of poor health, but he was kept informed of his team's progress as he underwent chemotherapy for the cancer that would ultimately claim his life in 2014. In his only season in charge, 2012–13, he saw Messi break another record: the most goals scored in a calendar year. It was a record held by Gerd Müller, who scored eighty-five for Bayern Munich and Germany in 1972. Messi finished the year with ninety-one, seventy-nine of them for Barcelona. Müller admitted: 'He's fantastic. He only has one defect and that is that he doesn't play for Bayern Munich!' With such figures, it came as no surprise that Messi was crowned world player for the fourth successive year, attracting nearly forty-two per cent of the votes, with Cristiano Ronaldo in second place again.

The earlier than expected elimination from the Copa América in 2011 was perhaps the key to Messi developing at such a rate in the season that followed. The false nine position that Messi had thrust upon him required an active and refreshed mind; even twenty-four year olds get tired. Messi had a tendency during the winter break to head back to Rosario and do nothing football-related for the whole period. He put on some weight during his time away, but having shed the excess, he embarked on a scoring streak that may never be bettered.

There was also a shift in the way Barcelona played. Cesc Fàbregas was signed from Arsenal in the summer of 2011, a player who had started his career at La Masia and was fully in tune to the Barça way even after seven years in North London. Fàbregas also liked to play in the free role between midfield and attack. But his acquisition did nothing to disrupt Messi's flow, and in fact enhanced Messi's already impressive record. After all, few teams knew how to stem the tide once Messi and Barcelona's passing movements clicked into gear.

It was the variety of goals scored by Messi during Guardiola's last season, rather than just the number, that emphasised how much of a shift there had been in his positional play and ability to create danger from different parts of the pitch. Teams were using two markers in failed attempts to stop him. He would simply drop deeper and create space for his teammates to surge into. Messi had evolved so much as a player and finisher that he now had answers in whichever part of the pitch he found himself. Eight of the seventy-three goals he scored for Barça that season came from his weaker right foot, six were lobbed finishes inside the penalty area. The trademark Messi goal was the cut-in from the right with a low left-foot finish. For the fourth successive year he was the top scorer in the Champions League. Messi also seemed to be excused those interminable runs that all strikers endure, when the ball just will not go in. In 2010, he went 474 minutes without scoring, or

Skills pay the bills – the enthusiasm for playing
has always been at the heart of Messi's game.

Relax and rebirth

just over five games. In 2011–12, he scored in ten consecutive games, and managed to find the net in seven straight games on the road. These records seem all the more impressive when you consider he was the most fouled player in the world, his progress stopped illegally on 134 occasions. Of the 317 shots he attempted that season, more than half were on target. His durability was never in doubt: he started fifty-seven of the sixty games he played and was never substituted. He was Barcelona's talisman, their main man and their iron man.

Some observers believe that the teams in the lower reaches of the Primera División do not provide stern enough opposition for those at the sharp end, and that this somehow lessens the quality and merit of what Messi has achieved. However, that argument does not take into account the pressure that comes with playing for Barcelona. Their brand of football is different: it is patient, high-possession, fast-moving and fascinating to watch. It may look easy and relaxed but it requires all eleven players, including the goalkeeper, to be finely tuned and not prone to error. Even with the weight of goals stacked so firmly in his favour, it is incumbent on Messi to show he has the confidence to do better than before. It is why so many of his goals come in the final fifteen minutes of matches. He knows he needs to continue to show the desire, the hunger that is required to make Barcelona such a force. It is why he takes the penalties, the free-kicks. He wants to underline that he is willing to take responsibility. It is why he continues to take penalties even after he has missed.

It was this decisive, confident form that made the 2012–13 league campaign Barcelona's most dominant yet. They finished it with one hundred points, leading the Primera División from round one through to round thirty-eight, and capturing the title with nearly a month to spare. Of their 115 goals in the league, Messi scored forty-six, and twelve of his passes led to goals for others. In all he contributed sixty goals for Barcelona, eight of them in the Champions League, where he added three further assists.

Barcelona were as dominant in the Champions League in moving through to the latter stages as they were at home. Since 2008,

Barça had always reached the last four, and this 2012–13 season was no different. However, anyone predicting a Barça–Real final was to be disappointed. The German teams Bayern Munich and Borussia Dortmund had other ideas. Jürgen Klopp's Dortmund knocked out Real 4–3 on aggregate. But that narrow win was nothing compared to the carnage that took place when Barça travelled to Munich for the first leg. Munich did everything to Barça that Barça normally do to teams, but with more speed and just as clinically. Two goals from Thomas Müller, and one each from Mario Gómez and Arjen Robben, did not flatter Bayern. They had fourteen shots on the night, eleven of them on target. The saddest sight was a clearly unfit Messi on the fringes of the game, having sustained a hamstring injury in the previous round against Paris Saint-Germain. He was clearly not totally fit. But as coaches had found before, telling Leo he cannot play is not the easiest thing to do.

The injury was serious enough that he played no part in the return leg when Barcelona were taught another lesson, losing 3–0. Four days later, Barça wrapped up their twenty-second league title, but the celebrations felt a touch bittersweet. The manner of their European exit, 7–0 on aggregate, had opened wounds. Their football looked pedestrian and dated, and it looked like an injured Messi's career had reached a crossroads. For the second successive European semi-final, Barça had been outplayed. There were mitigating circumstances, not least that this Bayern side would go on and win the title and dominate German football for the next three years as well as providing the bulk of the German World Cup-winning side. And, significantly, Barcelona had been without their manager for three months of the season. Vilanova had been missing from the bench from the middle of December 2012 until March 2013 while he undertook a course of chemotherapy for throat cancer. At the end of the season he resigned, keenly aware that the pressures of such a high-profile job were not compatible while recovering from the illness. Vilanova passed away in April 2014 after a relapse.

Putting aside the tragedy, Barcelona's league campaign had been nearly faultless. But on the grander stage, there were visible cracks

MOST FOULED

Odion Ighalo. Most fouled player (42) in the Premier League 2015–16

Lionel Messi. Fouled 16 more times (58) in La Liga 2015–16

appearing. To get back to the style of 2009 and 2011, and the winning ways of 2012–13, a change was required. The relationship between Messi and manager has always been crucial to his performance. The five years he worked under Guardiola and Vilanova had shaped the kind of player he had become. The next appointment, though, was not to come from within the camp. There had been rumours that Luis Enrique, now the head of Barcelona B, was being considered for the job, but in the end they plucked Gerardo Martino from Newell's Old Boys. His brand of football was attractive to those in the Barcelona hierarchy, and he was more than aware of what Messi meant to the club and had his own ideas about how he would get the most out of his fellow Argentine.

Not for the first time, however, there were rumblings about Messi's future. The Premier League was the most likely destination with Manchester City's wealthy owners apparently prepared to pay whatever it took to take the player to England. Wages would not be a problem. 'Messi is only still at Barcelona because he promised it to Tito Vilanova at his deathbed,' Henk ten Cate, a former coach at Camp Nou, told *De Telegraaf* newspaper in Holland. The veracity of that quote may be questioned, but after eight years of playing for the same club, the thought must have popped into Messi's head that now was the time to escape the Barcelona bubble. Two of his closest friends in the Argentina national side, Sergio Agüero and Pablo Zabaleta, could give him the low-down on life at the Etihad. They had ended a long wait to win the league title in 2012 and were now looking to conquer Europe and beyond.

Not that Barcelona were going to hand over their position easily. Rather than an outgoing global superstar, they added another to their roster in the shape of Brazilian striker Neymar. He played his club football at Santos, Pelé's old club, and had been scoring at a rate of a goal every other game. Real Madrid were also interested, but when they were rebuffed turned their attention to Welshman Gareth Bale, paying a world record fee of around one hundred million euros. When Neymar scored one of Brazil's goals in beating world champions Spain in the Confederations Cup, there were concrete assurances that Barça had done some good business.

Subsequent years would prove that Messi and Neymar were a good fit, but there was not an instant chemistry. Neymar could only manage fifteen goals in all competitions in his debut season in La Liga. More puzzling was how Messi's figures had dropped: he scored just forty-one goals in all competitions. In the aftermath of that 2013–14 season, Messi gave the rarest of things: a public declaration that he would stay at Camp Nou for as long as the fans wanted him. Maybe it was his way of saying he was aware of the rumours about his future. There was ambiguity in his words, but at the start of the next season he was still in Catalonia.

Messi was not helped by a series of injuries in the 2013–14 season. He had enjoyed four relatively injury-free seasons under Guardiola. Some of that was down to coaching, but he had also altered the way he lived away from the pitch. He had grown into his body, understanding what moves it could make, positioning himself to receive the ball in areas where the body would be placed under the least amount of pressure. But now, at the age of twenty-six, with his club needing him as much as ever, he suffered three separate injuries before Christmas. Barcelona coped surprisingly well in his absence, hanging on to the top spot for much of the first half of the season. Although Martino said he would change nothing that had made Barcelona successful, there were crucial technical introductions that affected Barcelona's main man. Notably, the coach asked the full-backs to play a less expansive game, to hold back at times. In previous years, the likes of right-back Dani Alves had been a marauding threat, almost playing as an orthodox right-winger. His runs would create space for the likes of Messi and David Villa to exploit. Without the constant running of Alves, and a similar outlet on the left provided by either Jordi Alba or Adriano, Barcelona started to look slightly more prosaic and workmanlike. It was likely that Martino believed the defeat at the hands of Bayern the previous season was due to a sometimes reckless adherence to the principles they had relied on for half a decade.

HELPING TO STRIKE

In the 2015-16 season, Messi assisted 16 of his teammates' goals, with 9 made to fellow striking force, Luis Suárez.

There were problems off the field for Messi as well. He was under investigation for tax fraud, something that would linger on in the background until summer 2016 before being resolved. He would later admit that it was a challenging time for him. Perhaps the fact that he was no longer performing superhuman feats regularly meant that for the first time since 2009, he did not receive the Ballon d'Or that year. It went to Ronaldo, who had a defining moment for his country when he scored four goals in a World Cup play-off match against Sweden. Messi finished second in the voting, but he had spent much of the three months before the award injured, and maybe that was why the huge number of goals he scored in the calendar year of 2013 was overlooked.

La Liga turned into a three-way race for the title. Atlético Madrid had built themselves up into a position to challenge Barça and Real, despite having to sell their best striker almost annually. In Diego Simeone, they had a coach with tactical nous, fire in his belly and an attachment to the club he managed, despite hailing from Argentina. Atlético crashed the cosy party, winning the league on the final day of the season at Camp Nou, when they prevented Barcelona gaining the win they needed. Simeone's side nearly won the Champions League that season, too, but they were beaten in the final by a Real side who finally got their hands on *La Decima*, their tenth title.

The finger was pointed at Martino for Barcelona's mini-slump and he paid for it with his job. Former Argentina manager César Luis Menotti perhaps summed up in retrospect the predicament for the man who tried but failed in his one year at the helm. 'Argentina, with Tata Martino', he said in 2016, 'has become a team which represents his ideas, something he could not do at Barcelona as their style is non-negotiable'.

So Martino exchanged Barcelona for Argentina, and Barça went back to the future with their next appointment: Luis Enrique, the former midfielder who had been in charge of the B team. With the arrival of a new manager and new players there was a belief around Camp Nou that things might start to change. Not that Messi was going to change. Just evolve.

'THE FLEA' THAT DRIBBLES

Messi's skill with the ball is such that it often looks
as if the ball is stuck to his feet. Here his dribble
rate shows his success in dribbling to striking glory.

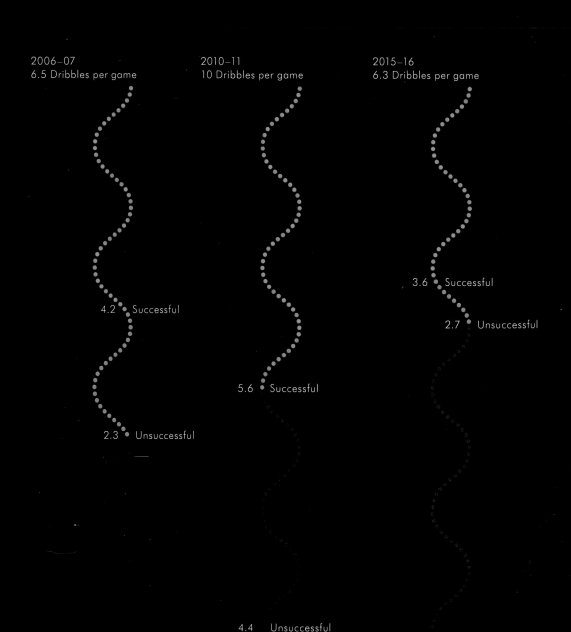

2006–07
6.5 Dribbles per game

4.2 Successful

2.3 Unsuccessful

2010–11
10 Dribbles per game

5.6 Successful

4.4 Unsuccessful

2015–16
6.3 Dribbles per game

3.6 Successful

2.7 Unsuccessful

Fastest dribblers

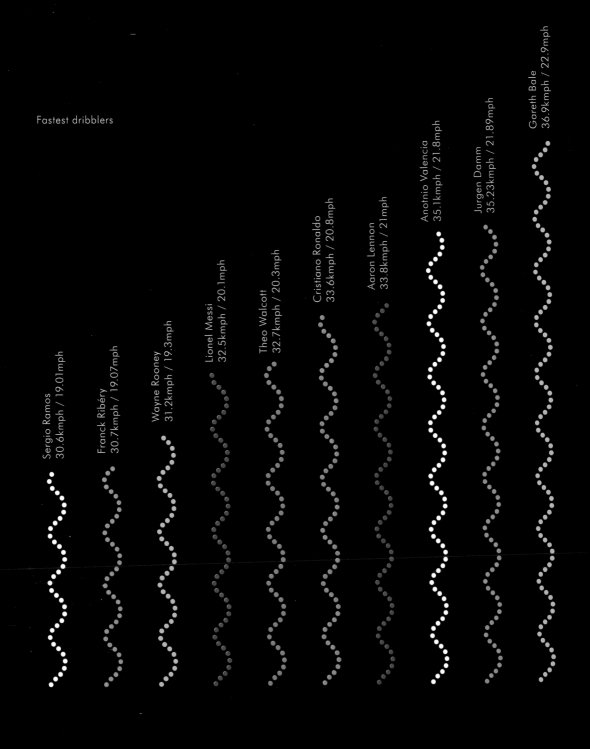

Sergio Ramos
30.6kmph / 19.01mph

Franck Ribéry
30.7kmph / 19.07mph

Wayne Rooney
31.2kmph / 19.3mph

Lionel Messi
32.5kmph / 20.1mph

Theo Walcott
32.7kmph / 20.3mph

Cristiano Ronaldo
33.6kmph / 20.8mph

Aaron Lennon
33.8kmph / 21mph

Anotnio Valencia
35.1kmph / 21.8mph

Jurgen Damm
35.23kmph / 21.89mph

Gareth Bale
36.9kmph / 22.9mph

Relax and rebirth

THE CHAMPIONS AGAIN – OF EVERYTHING

9

> 6
>
> **MESSI SPENDS THE MATCH MAKING A MENTAL X-RAY OF EVERY SPACE, EVERY MOMENT.**
>
> 9
>
> **Pep Guardiola**

The 2013–14 season had not been a happy time for player or club. With older players coming to the end of their time, it was hard to escape the notion that Barcelona were a club in transition. At the age of twenty-seven, Lionel Messi had a lot more football left in his legs. The same was not true of some of his teammates who had enjoyed the good times with him. The central defender Carles Puyol retired and the peerless midfield playmaker Xavi announced that the upcoming season would be his last at Camp Nou. Arguably he had been the most important player in the rebirth of Barcelona before Lionel Messi took the Catalans to a new level. Also leaving were Cesc Fàbregas and Alexis Sánchez, both heading for the Premier League, while goalkeeper Víctor Valdés was released. Valdés had been an essential part of the team's style, playing as a sweeper-keeper and dictating the tempo of play.

In their place came eight players, but there was one who stood out. If you judged Luis Suárez purely on his talent, he was the closest thing to Messi available. The twenty-seven year old averaged two goals every three games and was established as Uruguay's best player. He could create goals as well. The one problem that followed him around was that he was as notorious for his transgressions on the pitch as his striking prowess. At Ajax, he was banned for seven games for biting an opponent. There were further bans in England, for racially abusing Manchester United's Patrice Evra and then for biting Branislav Ivanovic of Chelsea. He then proved the previous incidents were no accident during the 2014 World Cup when he sank his teeth into Italy's Giorgio Chiellini. The four-month ban he received prevented him even training with his club side. His first game would be on 24 October 2014. When he had bitten Chiellini, he was a Liverpool player. By the time he had served his time, he was at Barcelona.

For years there was a sense of pride among Catalans that they had not gone down the Real Madrid route and hired *galacticos*. Now, though, it seemed Barcelona had adopted the Real model of bringing in star names. In consecutive seasons they had signed Suárez and Neymar for fees totalling nearly 170 million euros. Neymar's arrival had not been an unqualified success and there were questions about whether it had helped Messi. The Brazilian was fast, quicker maybe than any of his teammates, but his style seemed at odds with how Barcelona liked to control games. Suárez's addition meant there were three superstars up front, and the concern was whether they would be able to play seamlessly together as Barça players should.

The focus on Suárez's debut took some of the pressure away from Messi, Neymar and Luis Enrique. Not that there seemed to be many issues during the new manager's start with seven wins from eight league games, and the only defeat coming in a Champions League group match against the big-spending Paris Saint-Germain. As fate would have it, Suárez's league debut was an El Clásico on 25 October at the Bernabéu. Barça suffered their first league defeat, and when they lost again the week after there were suddenly storm clouds gathering above Camp Nou. The press claimed the three players could not play together: in 180 minutes only Neymar had managed to find the net. The team quickly returned to winning ways and by Christmas they were still in the hunt for three trophies: La Liga, Copa del Rey and Champions League.

However, Barcelona started 2015 with a defeat at Real Sociedad when both Messi and Neymar started on the bench, and neither looked particularly interested when they came on. There were now serious suggestions that Messi would be sold in the summer, having not been able to form any kind of relationship with Enrique. Messi missed training on the Monday after the game and that prompted Xavi to have a less-than-quiet word in The Flea's ear. Legend has it that he told Messi that unless he changed his attitude, Cristiano Ronaldo would win the Ballon d'Or again. The exchange might even have contained the odd expletive.

That dose of reality from one of his long-time teammates was the wake-up call Messi needed and made him wonder if there was something he could be doing differently to benefit the team. In a conversation with Enrique, Messi suggested he should go back to his former position on the right side of a front three, allowing Suárez to play through the middle. It was a selfless act. For more than five years, Messi had played at the apex of the attack, scoring two hundred goals there. It had not stopped him creating goals, either. Yet he could see that with Suárez through the middle, with his relentless running and energy, Barcelona could be unstoppable again. It might even allow more room for him to roam around, too. The change clicked, the triplet were liberated and 'MSN' (Messi, Suárez, Neymar) was born. It was a necessary move. With so much tactical analysis of opponents' strengths and weaknesses, it seemed that teams had finally realised how they could render Messi relatively impotent. The positional rethink might have been at his urging to help his teammates, but it had a positive effect on him, too. It sharpened his appetite for the game and he relished the new challenges, the new space to work in.

The proof of the pudding was in the eating, and a rejuvenated Messi finished the season with fifty-eight goals from fifty-seven games in all competitions. He created 143 chances with twenty-seven of them resulting in a goal. In fact, his statistics bore a remarkable similarity to those of 2011–12. Messi had found a way to maintain his output while sharing forward duties with others. Other partners had come and gone, the likes of Zlatan Ibrahimović and David Villa, but perhaps now, with his body no longer able to twist and turn as regularly, he seemed happier to share the burden of being Barça's main man.

All of a sudden, from looking like they were sleepwalking

PERCENTAGE OF TOUCHES Champions League Final 2009

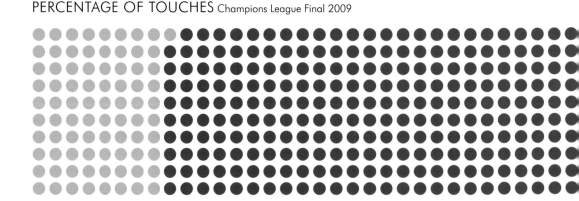

through the season, another treble seemed possible. By a quirk of fate, Barcelona were once again drawn against Bayern Munich in the Champions League. The difference this time was that Bayern were now coached by Pep Guardiola. The teacher was going to meet the pupil. As Messi told the press the day before the game when asked about his former boss: 'I have kept everything I learnt with him.' The first leg of the semi-final was at Camp Nou. Seeking to put the Catalans under immediate pressure, Bayern played a very high line, which the MSN frequently exposed. Only the agility of Manuel Neuer prevented an early goal. Guardiola then did what so many teams used to do to his Barcelona sides: he instructed his charges to sit deep and soak up the pressure. The tactic worked and deep into the second half the game was still goalless.

Seventy-six minutes of patient, but fruitless football had elapsed before Messi received the ball on the right side, thirty yards out. There was no imminent danger, there was not an opening, not unless you had the instincts of a panther. With little apparent back-lift, Messi arrowed in a left-foot shot with such power and swerve that it torpedoed into the net. Even the great Neuer could do nothing about it. But if that strike was stupendous in its simplicity and execution, the second three minutes later showed that Messi's range of skills was

● Barcelona touched the ball 673 times during the match.
● Messi was responsible for 81 of these, 12% of Barcelona's total.

The champions again – of everything

above that of any other player. It started from a similar position on the field, but this time he was faced with just one defender. Bayern giant Jérôme Boateng did the smart thing and showed Messi inside to take him further away from goal. But Messi was not scared of using his right foot. He dribbled, left Boateng on his backside, and seeing Neuer rush from his goal applied the deftest of chips into the net.

In injury time, desperately seeking an away goal, Bayern committed too many men forward. All three of the MSN were involved in the decisive third goal. Suárez dribbled the ball out of defence before being fouled. Messi took the free kick and spotted a sprinting Neymar. The Brazilian beat Neuer as emphatically as his teammate had twice before. 'There are no words for Messi. Just watch him and enjoy', said Barcelona goalkeeper Marc-André ter Stegen. It happened to be Messi's one-hundredth Champions League appearance. He had scored seventy-eight goals in them, which put him just ahead of Cristiano Ronaldo. The two would flip-flop the record over the years, so bragging rights never lasted that long. Guardiola was suitably impressed, even in defeat. He said: 'Messi is unstoppable. In this form, you can't stop him. He is used to all sorts of defenders. At the moment no one can stop him, he's too good. You just have to try to limit him, stop the ball reaching him, but even then you can't stop him.'

The MSN were back at it in the second leg. Messi fed Suárez, who in turn found Neymar, as Barcelona romped to a 5–3 aggregate victory. It was some manner of revenge for the mauling two years before. What was also noticeable was that this Barcelona side was not obsessed with always having the ball. In both games they had less of the ball than Bayern. Modern coach-speak often talks about being good in the 'transition' – the ability to spring from defence to attack. What no one believed possible was that Messi could find a way to be effective with two pacey forwards working in tandem ahead of him. He had found another dimension.

Guardiola would have seen it for himself when he allowed himself a rare night out to watch Barcelona put the finishing touches to a 3–1 aggregate victory over Manchester City in the previous round. He would have seen his former pupil pull the strings all over the pitch as the home side registered a pretty comprehensive 1–0 home win. Messi's close control and dribbling prowess were as good as they have ever been, but the one other thing that set him apart was the ability to run at top speed, stop and then play the killer pass. Barcelona's lone goal came from Ivan Rakitic, but it all started with a cross-field pass by Messi. Television replays showed Guardiola watching from one of the cheaper seats, a smile on his face that seemed to say he did not know the full extent of the monster he had helped create. Maybe at that moment the realisation that Bayern could be facing Messi in the later rounds flashed across his mind. He knew then how hard it would be to stop his former charge because it was not just his goals that could hurt.

The MSN, the three kings – or just the best attacking trio in club history.

In La Liga, Messi and Barcelona timed their run perfectly. From 28 February 2015 to the end of the season, they won eleven of their thirteen league games to overtake Real Madrid at the top of the table. Included in that sequence were victories over both the Madrid clubs. At Camp Nou, Messi played a full part in a 2–1 victory over Real and his arch-rival Cristiano Ronaldo. This was the verdict of Andy West, writing for the BBC website: 'The Argentine delivered a perfect free-kick into the penalty box for Jérémy Mathieu's headed opener and was the chief string-puller as his team ran riot in the second period, producing an especially delightful pass to create a late chance for Jordi Alba. Despite hitting the bar, scoring and bursting into life for the final stages of the first half, Ronaldo endured a largely frustrating night and did nowhere near enough to assist his team's attempts to find a second-half leveller.'

It was not just the goals that highlighted Messi's high performance. The statistics showed just how influential he was, with seventy-seven touches compared to Ronaldo's fifty-two. Even though this Barcelona was being fashioned in a completely different way to the short-passing, tiki-taka-based methods that had taken them to a treble six years earlier, they were just as effective. They may have shared possession equally with Real on the night, but they created chances and Messi was at the hub of everything they were doing.

The last big hurdle was Atlético Madrid, the defending champions. To call them robust would not do them justice: they fought for every second of every minute to stop the opposition playing, and then initiated their own attacks. If a team was ever built in the image of its manager, then Atlético's snarling, aggressive and passionate style perfectly represented Diego Simeone. He was way too smart to fall for Barcelona's quick counter-attacking, and too aggressive for the short passing that Barcelona would fall back on if plan A was not working. This was the penultimate week of the season and the pressure was building on Barça. Real, who could still win the title, were in front at Espanyol. But in the sixty-fifth minute Barça went ahead. Messi, staying calm amid the frenetic pace at which Barça were being forced to play, picked the ball up just outside the penalty area. Ahead of him were seven Atlético defenders and the goalkeeper, and just two Barcelona attackers. The odds were not good. Messi played a pass to Pedro, who laid it off back to Messi, who weaved through a packed area. One touch to set and then a low, left-footed shot into the net. It was a goal that had been seen before, but this one decided the title. Significantly it came twelve months after Barça had missed the chance to win the league against the same opposition. It was somehow fitting that the team's top scorer should claim the goal.

Now all that remained was whether Barça could win the other competitions they were still in to repeat the 2009 treble. First up was the Copa del Rey final against Athletic Bilbao at Camp Nou. It included another memorable Messi goal. But before that he had combined to set up Neymar for a volley that would have been one of the goals of the season had a linesman, erroneously as it turned out, not put his flag up for offside. Messi was rarely ruffled, but he was visibly annoyed here, remonstrating with the official long after the incident. Some players lose their focus and discipline in such a moment. Or they could do what Messi did and take matters into their own hands. Just twenty minutes had gone and he had the ball on the right wing, forty-five or so yards out. He started twisting and turning, attracting three men to his path. He seemed to dribble in some kind of pattern, accelerating then stopping, before leaving all three in his wake. Another defender approached on the edge of the area, Messi went outside him and drilled a hard, rasping, left-footed shot past the goalkeeper. He had possession of the ball for thirteen mesmerising seconds and had beaten five of the opposition.

Messi was involved in the second goal, exchanging passes with Rakitic before Suárez's perfectly weighted pass set up Neymar. The third and final Barcelona goal showed just how complete a player Messi had become. Dani Alves reached the byline before crossing low into the penalty area where Messi arrived with a left-foot finish one would expect from a predatory striker. La Liga and the Copa del Rey in the bag, only Juventus stood in their way in the Champions League.

THE NIGHT OF FIVE

On a Wednesday night in March 2012, Barcelona hit the German side Bayer Leverkusen for seven and Lionel Messi scored five of them. While Barcelona failed to win the Spanish League or the Champions League that season, Messi would enjoy his greatest ever goal-scoring campaign within the Championship. This match epitomised his free-scoring nature during 2012.

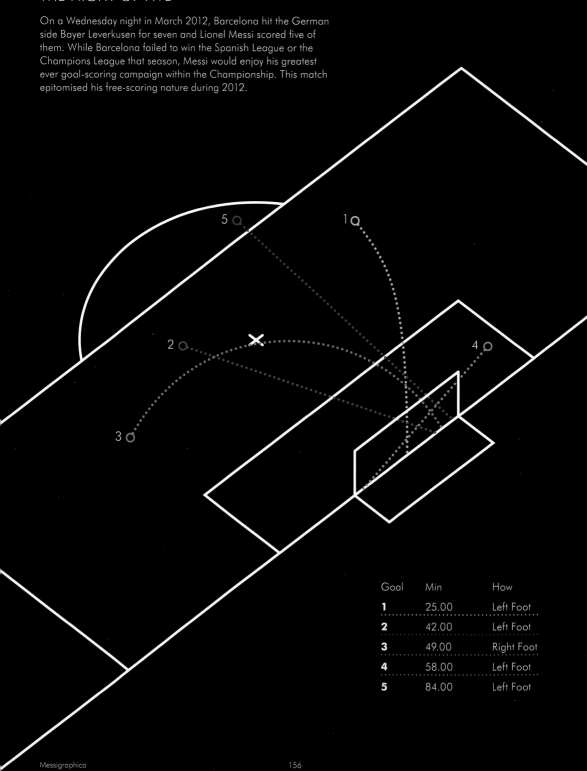

Goal	Min	How
1	25.00	Left Foot
2	42.00	Left Foot
3	49.00	Right Foot
4	58.00	Left Foot
5	84.00	Left Foot

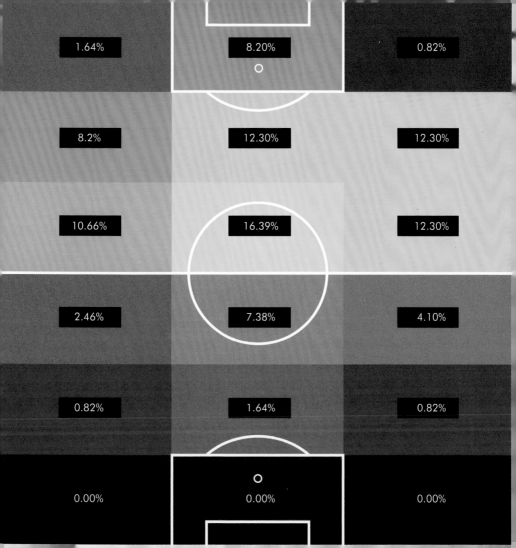

CHAMPIONS – AGAIN, AND AGAIN AND YET AGAIN

'

ONCE THEY SAID THEY CAN ONLY STOP ME WITH A PISTOL. TODAY YOU NEED A MACHINE GUN TO STOP MESSI.

'

Hristo Stoichkov

When Lionel Messi arrived at Camp Nou as a thirteen-year-old prodigy in 2000, Barcelona had won Europe's most important club trophy just once. That was back in 1992 when Ronald Koeman's extra-time free-kick silenced Sampdoria at Wembley. By the close of the 2014–15 season, they had won the European Cup, now rebranded the UEFA Champions League, four more times with the boy from Rosario playing major roles in the most recent three.

The Champions League always gets Messi's competitive juices going, just as playing on the grandest stages should for all great players. Despite the hours of practice, dedication in the gym, specially designed diets, and those secret moments when they perfect their free-kick techniques, a player's greatness comes down to a few important moments. It may not have required a study conducted by the Karolinska Institutet, the centre for medical research in Sweden, to underline why players lift their performance for the big games, it is just that they do. And Lionel Messi is no exception.

Champions League Final
27 May 2009
Barcelona 2–0 Manchester United
Rome

Manchester United, the defending champions, stood between Barcelona and their third European Cup/Champions League triumph. This was a great United team. They had been the best team in England since 2006 and seemed a good bet to become the first team to retain the European title in its modern form. They had strength in every area: Edwin van der Sar in goal, Nemanja Vidić and Rio Ferdinand in central defence, a midfield containing Paul Scholes and Ryan Giggs, and so many options up front, including Wayne Rooney and Cristiano Ronaldo. They were going to be no push-overs.

Only two players on the pitch were younger than Messi: teammate Sergio Busquets and the United midfielder Anderson. If there were fears that the little man might be intimidated by the atmosphere in the Olympic Stadium, his contributions during the opening fifteen minutes did little to change those pre-conceptions. Dropping deep, he would pick up the ball, dribble and usually find his progress derailed by the effervescent Park Ji-sung. But fifteen minutes is about all most teams can manage to subdue the tyro. In the nineteenth minute, responding to some typically strong, powerful running from Samuel Eto'o, he cut in from the right flank and hit a venomous, left-footed shot which rose too sharply. It was a warning.

By that stage, Barcelona had weathered a Ronaldo-inspired storm. They had also scored through Eto'o. Once Messi had his little run and shot, he seemed to remember that this Barcelona functioned when everyone played the role of orchestra conductor. There was a period in the first half when Barça had control of the ball for nearly

The night Messi soared into everyone's conscience – scoring the second goal against Manchester United in 2009.

Champions – again, and again and yet again

two minutes and Messi was involved five times. Only on one of those occasions did he choose to play a pass of incision, aware now that his teammates could do that difficult stuff just as well.

In the period from fifteen minutes to thirty, United began to learn a little more about the mini marvel. He went on dribbles, passing the ball before he was tackled. Three, maybe four, United players would try to use their physical strength to knock him to the ground. But while he may not have had the Adonis-like physique of Ronaldo on the other side, there was a toughness and street-like quality to the way Messi ran. It spoke of his earliest days, when he would play against his older, bigger brothers, and the first battle was to prove he was as good as them.

In the final fifteen minutes of the half, the smallest man on the pitch began to have a major impact. Messi showed why he was every opposing manager's nightmare because when he did not have the ball, he could be anywhere. On the left, on the right or through the middle. Barcelona may have played pretty triangles of passing, but when they tried to retrieve the ball from the opposition, they did so in gangs of four. This included Messi if the ball was in his zone. That his position was never fixed meant he was alive to anything within a twenty-yard radius. Because he was mainly central, and so much of the modern game was played through the middle, the ball was likely to end up frequently in his vicinity, especially as his teammates were so good at recycling possession. The effect was akin to watching a highly skilled boxer fighting an opponent who was more a puncher. In this game, United had attempted to land their heavy blows in the opening round. But when they were not put on the floor, Barcelona began to dominate and grew in confidence with every round. Messi's presence was that of a strong jab which could sometimes win rounds on its own. There seemed to be no limit to what that punch could do.

As the first half ended, Messi launched into one of his trademark surges down the United right. It was noticeable how Park, his shadow for the first twenty minutes, was some way from the action; it must have been exhausting marking someone whose movements were totally unpredictable. By the end of that opening forty-five minutes,

United looked as if they were out on their feet, and Messi looked as though he was just warming up. One down, Sir Alex Ferguson, the United manager, had options on the bench in Carlos Tevez and Dimitar Berbatov, and duly went for Tevez in place of Anderson. That meant Michael Carrick was left with the job in midfield of trying to contain Messi, Andrés Iniesta and Xavi. No one man was up to that.

Barcelona's play in the first fifteen minutes of the second half was so fluent, so appealing, that Messi was just one of half-a-dozen threats United had to deal with. Messi should have scored when Eto'o played a lovely ball across the six-yard box and Messi looked like he only had to slide it in. But John O'Shea tugged at the Argentine's shirt at the crucial moment, though the referee missed the obvious foul. But generally Messi was an onlooker during this spell. United had committed to attack, with Berbatov on for Park. Messi's big moment came when Ronaldo and Patrice Evra were sloppy in possession. The ball was picked up by Xavi, twenty-five yards from goal and with only Messi to aim for. The Argentine was on the left side of the penalty area, but the cross was almost perfect for the smallest player on the pitch. Messi's leap, with the ball slightly behind him, meant he headed the ball back across the goal. Van der Sar could only watch as the header floated past him and into the net. Even for a team like United, with a glorious history of comebacks, the game was up with twenty minutes left.

Messi was voted the fans' man of the match; Xavi was the UEFA man of the match. He had seen many big occasions in his career, other Champions League finals and a European Championship victory with his country. Messi, on the other hand, had not savoured this stage before, yet he had risen to the challenge and scored the game-ending goal. Seven years later, Messi would say the goal was his favourite: 'I always say that I consider the importance of the goal, more than for its beauty, and so mine would be the first I scored in a Champions League final, with a header, for the importance it had.'

Much had been made in the build-up to the game that Messi had never scored against an English team. He had now. He would score a few more in time. And he would do it again against Manchester United.

Torturing
Manchester United
again – Champions
League final, 2011.

Champions League final
28 May 2011
Barcelona 3–1 Manchester United
Wembley

Only two years had elapsed since their previous meeting in a
Champions League final, and the similarities were hard to ignore. Both
sides entered the contest as champions of their respective leagues. They
were both free-scoring units and there were fifteen men who started that
Rome contest in 2009. But while United did not have Cristiano Ronaldo
anymore, Barcelona still had Messi; an improved Messi, a Messi who

scored even more goals and who for the third successive year was the top scorer in the Champions League. In those intervening two years, the world had grown to know more about him, that he was not a flash in the pan, and barring injury that he would be a very important player. When the English commentator Clive Tyldesley described him as the best player in the world, there were few dissenting voices.

In 2009, Messi was very much the junior member of Pep Guardiola's preferred three-man forward line. Then, he was flanked by Samuel Eto'o and Thierry Henry. Now the pair had been replaced by David Villa and Pedro. The newcomers were brilliant in their own right, but there was no doubt they did not have the personality of the men they succeeded. After the opening exchanges at Wembley, one thing became apparent: Park Ji-sung was the man charged with stopping Messi's forays from deep, just as he had been in Rome until he became tired.

The opening ten minutes were frenetic. United were slightly on top but without threatening a goal. Messi's first meaningful contribution came when he exchanged passes with Villa, playing a ball through to the Spaniard who was tackled before he could shoot. There were passages of play where it was easy to see why Pedro and Villa were in the side as they switched positions with Messi in seamless fashion. Sometimes Messi dropped deep, sometimes he darted into the box. Either way, one of his teammates covered for him.

In the eighteenth minute, Messi went on a dribble that took out four United players and reminded them that they no longer had a player like him. Park was nowhere near him and the midfield duo of Giggs and Carrick were not nearly nimble enough to keep track. But everything was hunky-dory because there was a new fact doing the rounds: Messi had never scored in England. As if to prove there was substance to the statistic, he miscontrolled after playing a one-two with Villa that should have led to the opening goal. In fact, he had two more moments when he could have been more precise. No matter, Barcelona took the lead in the twenty-seventh minute when strike partner Pedro had all the time in the world to finish low and hard past van der Sar.

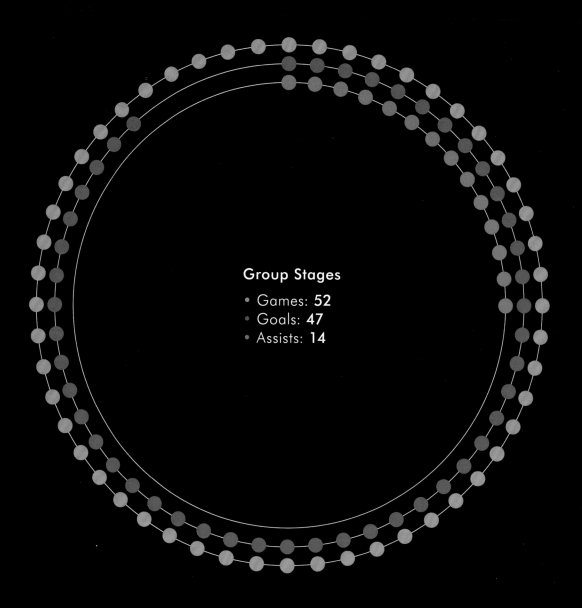

Group Stages
- Games: **52**
- Goals: **47**
- Assists: **14**

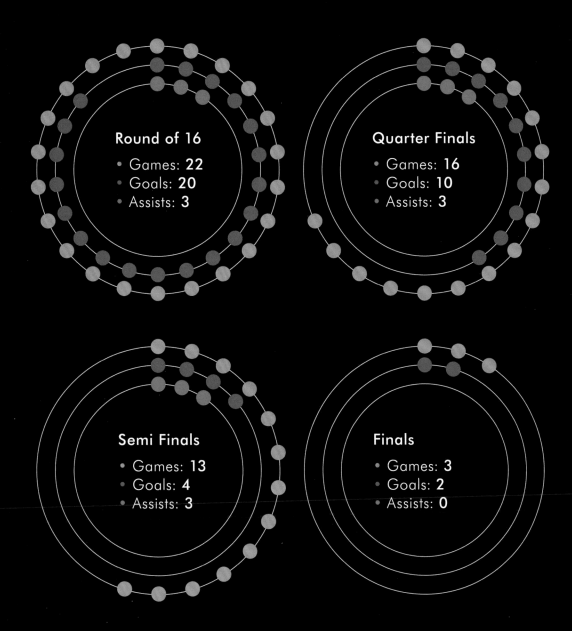

Round of 16
- Games: **22**
- Goals: **20**
- Assists: **3**

Quarter Finals
- Games: **16**
- Goals: **10**
- Assists: **3**

Semi Finals
- Games: **13**
- Goals: **4**
- Assists: **3**

Finals
- Games: **3**
- Goals: **2**
- Assists: **0**

Champions – again, and again and yet again

What was surprising was that for all their dominance, Barcelona had just a one-goal advantage. Then, even that was wiped out when Wayne Rooney started and ended a move in the thirty-fourth minute. Messi, though, had yet to make an impression on the game. United made sure their challenges on him were hard: twice Antonio Valencia dived in and left Messi on the floor. The hope was that he would stop showing for the ball, and that he would drift into areas where he could do no damage. It had not happened yet, but there seemed to be a mounting frustration enveloping Leo. His dribbles had not come to anything and he had yet to play a pass that threatened United's goal. That was summed up as the half drew to a close. Centrally, he picked up the ball and dribbled towards goal. Villa pulled off to the right and Messi released him. Villa squared the ball back for the onrushing Messi who was just too small to get a foot to the cross. He hung his head in despair.

The first half came to an end and it was generally agreed that it had been Xavi and Iniesta who had kept things ticking along rather than Messi. The little Argentine was perhaps guilty of overcomplicating, occasionally taking too many touches when just one would suffice. What became clear when the game restarted was that United were clinging on thanks to one moment of brilliance in the first half. Barcelona had enjoyed more than sixty-five per cent of possession and that figure seemed to be getting higher. The only touches United had were last-ditch blocks to prevent shots from Xavi or Iniesta finding the target.

Another chance came Messi's way at the start of the half. A Dani Alves shot was cleared as far as the edge of the box. Messi's attempted lob had to beat four defenders and the goalkeeper on its way to goal. It did not get past the head of the experienced Patrice Evra. Thwarted again, the levels of frustration were growing. He had scored fifty-two goals already that season; the game was normally a lot easier.

Another Barcelona attack started. They kept hold of the ball for twenty-five seconds and, unusually, Messi had not touched it once. And then he did. Fifty-three minutes had gone, and he was left of centre, maybe thirty yards out. United had the dribble well covered, with Evra,

Vidić and Ferdinand around the D of the penalty area. But Messi had already decided what he was going to do. He accelerated and swung back his left foot and hit a ferocious shot that swerved around Vidić and beat van der Sar before he had time to move. Messi had his goal, but his celebration was instructive. He sprinted to the advertising boards behind the goal, in front of the Barcelona fans, and kicked one of them. At that moment, elation and frustration were jointly released. It was his twelfth goal in the Champions League that season. And his first in England.

Messi's confidence had grown thanks to the goal, and he emphasised that in the sixty-third minute when he received the ball on the edge of the penalty area, and span on to his favoured left foot and shot. This time van der Sar blocked with his legs. Messi, though, looked in the mood. Barça were constructing moves that lasted more than a minute, when the only United player to touch the ball was their goalkeeper. It was beautiful to watch for the neutral, but for United it was torture. Their right-back Fábio went off with cramp, the sign of an overworked player. Yet twenty minutes remained.

The third goal, which ultimately finished the game as a contest, started with a Messi dribble down the United right. After he found his way past three opposition players, he lost control. The ball, though, was recycled to Villa on the edge of the area. Suddenly the ball was with Messi and he chose the dink into the top corner. It was a thing of beauty. There is a shot of Messi looking on when the ball rests in the net, on his knees celebrating.

The goal took the wind out of the game. Antonio Valencia received a yellow card for one of the six fouls perpetrated on Messi during the evening. Not one of them was malicious but all bore the hallmarks of the frustration that United had endured. At the end, the cameras were trained on two images: Guardiola and Ferguson sharing a genuine embrace, and then the joyous face of Lionel Messi. Only twenty-three, his face still with some puppy fat, but a player capable of making opponents scream like a baby. Barcelona's 'Dream Team' won their first European Cup at the old Wembley; it seemed a new dream team had been unveiled at the new stadium.

After the game Guardiola was moved to say: 'As I have said many times, Messi is the best player I have ever seen and perhaps the best player I will ever see. We played very well and have great players, but without him we would not be able to play the way we do. He gives us that extra cutting edge, a step-up in quality. We have hard work, talent and tactics that help the players feel comfortable, but Messi is unique, irreplaceable, impossible to duplicate.' Ferguson was also full of praise: 'We never controlled Lionel Messi, but many people have had to say that over the years.'

At the end of the final, Messi received UEFA's best-player-in-Europe trophy. With fifty-three goals scored across three competitions that season, there was no compelling argument for anyone else.

Champions League Final 2015
6 June 2015
Barcelona 3–1 Juventus
Berlin

In the week before the Champions League final of 2015, the focus had been on what game-plan Juventus would utilise to contain the MSN triumvirate of Messi, Suárez and Neymar. No one else had managed it for the best part of a season. In the wake of the 2011 Champions League final, Sir Alex Ferguson had talked of how every team had a cycle, natural evolution that meant the Barcelona side of that year could not sustain that level of brilliance. He was right to the extent that four years had passed before they reached the final again. Indeed, of the eleven who started that famous evening at Wembley, only six remained. Crucially, two of the new men were Luis Suárez and Neymar. Messi was no longer playing centrally, having moved back to the right to accommodate the Uruguayan. Xavi was now on the bench, his thirty-five-year-old legs finally showing signs of age.

For all the newly integrated brilliance of Suárez and Neymar, it was hard to work out where Messi fitted in. He had scored fifty-eight goals in the season going into the final in Berlin, a staggering amount for any player. Yet he no longer played the role of chief destroyer. There was still the lingering suspicion that as impressive as his goals tally was (he has scored forty or more goals each season since 2009) he had managed to accumulate them against sub-standard Spanish defences, defences who did not tackle as much as they did in the German, Italian or English leagues. Now, in this slightly more withdrawn role, he was less in the firing line for the physical warfare that went on in the middle of the pitch.

For the previous two seasons, Messi had surrendered the Ballon d'Or to Cristiano Ronaldo. Now, he had the chance to show that he was back to his searing best. The opposition was provided by Juventus, who just happened to have knocked out holders Real Madrid in the semi-final. The Italian champions also had the chance to do a treble of their own, just like Barcelona. Their aggressive, counter-pressing style was similar to the one favoured by Atlético Madrid, so might pose Barcelona problems. Even so, Barça were huge favourites.

The bookmakers' odds looked justified when they went ahead in the fourth minute. It started with Messi, who spotted Jordi Alba marauding down the left. Alba played some one-touch passes with Neymar, before Andrés Iniesta played an astute pass for Ivan Rakitic to finish off a frighteningly swift move. The goal gave the impression that Juventus could not live with Barça when they hit top gear. Messi and Neymar had been involved, but very much on the periphery. But the fact that the Spanish side had possession of the ball for a minute before striking, that eight members of the team had touched the ball during the course of the move, and that the first Juventus player to touch it was when Gianluigi Buffon picked it out of the net, made fans of the Old Lady fearful of what might happen next. Neutrals wondered if this could turn out to be the exhibition they had dreamt of.

One of the side-issues to the game was the meeting between Patrice Evra and Suárez. The pair were once embroiled in an unsavoury clash in a Liverpool versus Manchester United Premier League match in 2011, which resulted in the Uruguayan being fined and banned for eight games for racially abusing the Frenchman. Suárez never apologised and there remained bad blood between the two. However,

Evra must have wished his nemesis had been playing on the right of Barcelona's three in Berlin. Instead it was Messi, hitting diagonal balls for Neymar or drifting in, allowing Dani Alves to exploit the space. The Argentine was showing that he was just as effective out wide where he was consolidating one side of the pitch for the Spanish side. Together with Alves, he exchanged 143 passes during the course of the game. All but sixteen found their intended target. Given that the pair were up against Paul Pogba and Evra made the figures all the more impressive.

This was an accomplished Juventus side, nonetheless, and included in their ranks Andrea Pirlo, Carlos Tevez and maybe the best goalkeeper of the previous generation in Buffon. They could mix it or play flair football, and in Massimo Allegri they had a coach with an enormous depth of experience. As they took a grip on the game, so Messi was in danger of becoming marginalised. Sensing this, the Argentine drifted inside and took the ball-winning burden from his teammates by inviting challenges while in possession. The 2015 Barcelona side probably ran more than some of the previous incarnations and could do with a breather. Messi only ran as much as he had to. He could be seen in this game, forty yards from goal, tempting Pogba or Claudio Marchisio to take the ball off him, before laying it off to Busquets or Alves. Messi was no longer the young tyro, but one of the elder statesman of the team. Only Iniesta had spent longer in the first team than him. Before the first half ended, he left

Juve with a reminder of the danger and havoc he could wreak when he dribbled from thirty yards out, seemingly past the entire Italian defence. The only thing that defeated him was the confines of the pitch. It showed Juventus that even when they had dealt with the speed and power of Neymar and Suárez, the guy on the right needed marshalling as well.

In the fifty-first minute, he dictated a move with the other members of the MSN that threatened to end the game. One-twos with Neymar and then Suárez took him from the right side of the penalty area to the left. No Juve player got close to him. The shot, though, was just as distant. However, this period of intense domination was interrupted by a Juventus equaliser from Alvaro Morata. As Barcelona's grip on the game seemed to be slipping, Messi stepped forward. Picking the ball up on the halfway line, perhaps sensing that as a senior player it was his job to galvanise, he drove at the Juventus defence. Suddenly, this was the twenty-year-old Messi, with wings on his heels and magic in his boots. He could not be stopped, and as he approached the left side of the area he shot low and hard. Buffon threw a hand to parry the ball. But the escape was only momentary as Suárez hammered home the rebound.

There were still twenty minutes to go, but from then until the end of the game Messi enjoyed himself. The situation was perfect with Juventus committed to attack. In the seventh minute of injury time, Messi played the pass that started the counter-attack for the third goal, scored by Neymar. He had been involved in every goal, though Iniesta was voted man of the match.

Messi gave his own humble opinion of himself after the game. 'I prefer to win titles with the team ahead of individual awards or scoring more goals than anyone else', he said. 'I'm more worried about being a good person than being the best football player in the world. When all this is over, what are you left with? When I retire, I hope I am remembered for being a decent guy.' Others preferred to dwell on him as a player. 'He is back, he is there where I had the privilege to train him... I compare him with Pelé', said Pep Guardiola. Teammate Sergio Busquets said: 'Messi is a guarantee. He's the best player in the world, even if he doesn't get the awards. Everyone in football knows.'

In Guardiola's eleven, Messi was the main man, playing centrally and drifting only occasionally. In 2015, he became the danger-man from the right, moving wherever he saw he could inflict pain from this flank.

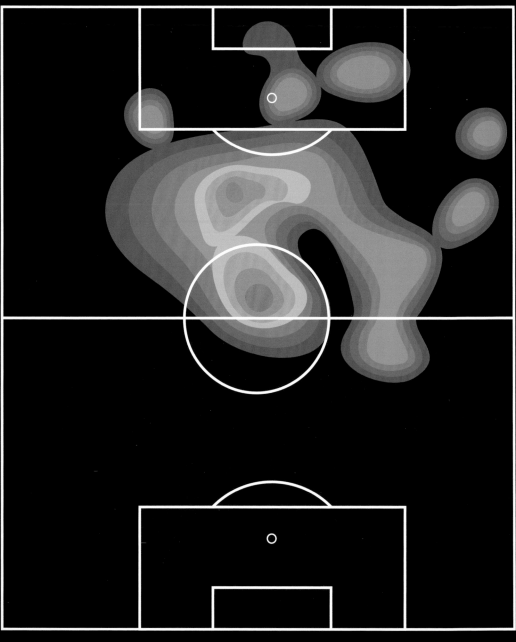

2011 Final

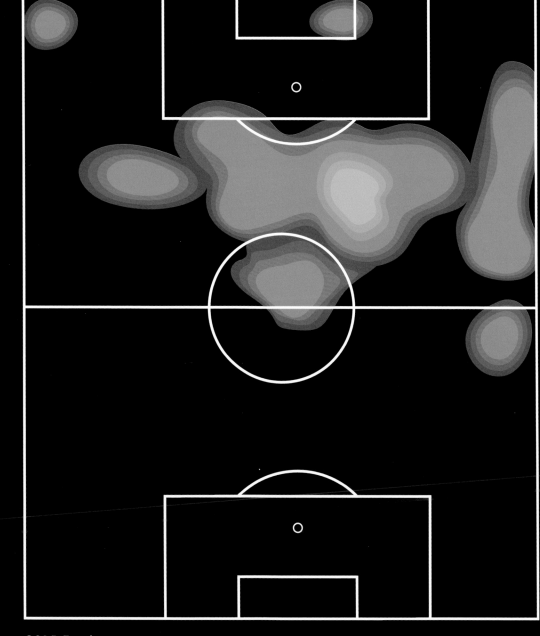

2015 Final

BACK TO THE FUTURE

11

'

THE TROUBLE IS THAT WE'VE SEEN SO MUCH OF MESSI THAT WE THINK HE'S NORMAL. I CAN'T UNDERSTAND HOW A PLAYER HAS GOT TO THAT LEVEL. THE TEAM ARE TRAINED BETTER, TACTICALLY THEY'RE BETTER, PSYCHOLOGICALLY THEY'RE BETTER. AND MESSI IS THE REFERENCE, BUT HE'S SURROUNDED BY TOP-QUALITY PLAYERS WHO MAKE HIM BETTER.

,

Luis Enrique speaking in late 2015

At the start of the 2015–16 season, Lionel Messi found himself back to where he had been in 2009. Standing at the summit of football's Mount Olympus, he must have been keenly aware that in 2015 greatness was scrutinised on a week-by-week, game-by-game basis. Show any sign that you were not where you used to be and your place would be taken by someone who wanted it more. It was a battle that he was used to: throughout his ascent to the top, Cristiano Ronaldo had been the gauge of how good he was. The Portuguese had been driven by the same ambition. When their duel started, they were both young men. But the Real Madrid player was now in his thirties and Messi could see that he was also approaching the latter stage of his career. But on the flip side, he was playing in a young side, where key players such as Neymar, Jordi Alba and Sergio Busquets were still in their early or mid-twenties. Where once he was the young star, there was youth within the team, who would take it through the mid-stage of the decade and beyond. He had shown during the previous year that he was willing to change his position to accommodate new talent, in the shape of Luis Suárez. His job now was to make sure that the club's massive investment in the Uruguayan and Neymar bore fruit.

The first task of the season was to reclaim the European Super Cup, the trophy competed for by the Champions League winners and the holders of the Europa League. It may have been a match too far in terms of importance, but it still provided Barça with their first silverware of the season, courtesy of a 5–4 extra-time win against Sevilla. It was a match in which they were behind and then rebounded to lead 4–1. Pedro scored the winning goal, his final contribution to the Catalan club before being sold to Chelsea. But others will remember that night in Tbilisi for the two exquisite free-kicks scored by the number ten. For so long, the responsibility of taking charge of set-pieces had been Leo's, even with the acquisition of Suárez, who was famed for his dead-ball ability at Liverpool. Messi took them all, whether through design, desire or seniority. He once gave an insight into the amount of time and effort expended on practising free-kicks. 'We work on how to move so that the ball goes to the right place', he said, 'and also you learn things over the course of your career. I like to hit the ball over the players' wall, but from time to time I like to mix it up a little bit so that the goalkeeper doesn't know where I'm going. I want to keep him confused until I kick. I like to keep the goalkeeper in doubt.'

Nine minutes separated Messi's two free-kick goals in the Georgian capital. Both went to his right, the goalkeeper's left. There was enough disguise that Portuguese stopper Beto, who had trained with Cristiano Ronaldo, could not get close to either. The legend of Messi's ability with the ball was enhanced that season when a video was released of him in training, finding the net after kicking the ball a full twenty yards behind the goal-line, shaping the ball like a boomerang. Even his teammates, used to seeing him do incredible things on the practice ground and in matches, were left open-mouthed.

Ronald Koeman, who scored Barcelona's winner in the 1992 European Cup final from a dead-ball, held the club record for most free-kick goals with twenty-three. Messi was closing in on that record and the countdown was another sub-plot in what would turn out to be another successful season for him and Barcelona. However, it did not start that well. The hint of vulnerability exposed by Sevilla almost became a full-scale crisis when a full-strength Barcelona lost the first leg of the Spanish Super Cup 4–0 to Athletic Bilbao. Messi scored the goal in the return leg that finished in a 1–1 draw. Four straight wins in La Liga were followed by two defeats, including a 4–1 reverse at Celta Vigo, with two goals by Iago Aspas, a player deemed not good enough for Liverpool reserves.

Even worse was to follow for Messi. In the early stages of a league game against Las Palmas he sustained a knee injury. Throughout his career there had been concerns about whether his knees could sustain the weight of the incredible series of pivots he asked them to perform. A scan confirmed a ligament problem that kept him out for two months, missing the majority of Barcelona's Champions League group matches. Not since the metatarsal injury in 2006 had the Argentine spent so long on the sidelines. Now twenty-eight, there were genuine fears that this knee injury might herald the beginning of the end.

Messi had been in the Barça first team for more than ten years and his body was under incredible pressure. The nature of Barcelona's change in style meant he was being asked to play a more expansive game, with less time for in-game recuperation. Since 2005, he had only had three summers' rest, with the demands of international football meaning he represented Argentina in World Cups, Olympic Games and Copa Américas. Three Champions League victories also meant long trips to represent Barcelona in the Club World Cup. He was approaching five hundred appearances for Barcelona and six hundred games in all. Few professionals reach that mark until they are well into their thirties. If Messi had a problem, it was that his personality on the field rarely betrayed him. He never seemed tired, rarely moaned if a pass intended for him was misplaced. Any interviews he gave rarely suggested a player who felt the burden of being the world's best. The indelible image of him was with a smile on his face.

Time for a break – Messi has not had a summer off since 2013.

However, at the start of the 2015–16 season rumours of a Messi departure began to re-surface. The club president Josep Bartomeu responded to questions by saying: 'He does not want to go, he is happy, but he suffers a lot of pressure not just on the pitch but also away from it.' When a president speaks, it is usually in response to a genuine concern. Stories of a potential departure had not gone away since Manchester City hired Barcelona's former director of football, Txiki Begiristain. These tales of disquiet increased when City secured the services of Pep Guardiola in the summer of 2016, along with reports that Messi's relationship with his current coach did not suggest they were dining companions. At the start of 2015, the pair had cleared the air for the good of the team. But Luis Enrique's praise for the last two letters of the MSN triumvirate after the Champions League victory was noticeable. However, Enrique had played a key part in making sure the Argentine did not suffer burnout at the start of the season, his busy schedule compounded by the pressure of having to play two Argentina friendlies. Even so, maybe this essentially shy, homespun boy, did finally want to taste what it was like to play in another country. He had asked, it was said, fellow Argentines Sergio Agüero and Pablo Zabaleta what the weather was like in Manchester.

However, he seemed to put an end to those rumours in an interview he gave to the French publication *France Football*. He said: 'I have always said that Barcelona is my home and that I want to retire at this club, but I was talking about my European career there. I could never play for another European club than Barcelona. But I would like to play in Argentina, because I left when I was still little. I would like to know how it is to be part of the Argentine game. Anything can happen in football, but I have no doubts about what I want, and what I want is to stay here at Barcelona.'

Messi was finally passed fit for a substitute role in the first El Clásico of the season on 21 November. Barça ran riot that night, with goals from Suárez, Neymar and Iniesta giving the visitors clear daylight before Messi was introduced. Cameras had shown an exhilarated Messi celebrating every goal on the bench, his admiration for his teammates clearly genuine. In the half-hour afforded him he set up chances for Suárez and Neymar, before being involved in the fourth goal, finished by the Uruguayan. The final score was 0–4, a result that would play a key part in the sacking of Rafael Benítez as Real coach six weeks later.

Messi's absence had not been as keenly felt as might be expected. Before the game, Suárez and Neymar had scored twenty goals between them. However, there was never any doubt that Messi would walk back into the team, and a week later he scored his first league goal since the injury. By that stage he had already played in Barça's 6–1 mauling of Roma in the Champions League. He scored twice that night, the first of the goals after a twenty-four-pass move that showcased all the talents of the rebuilt Barcelona. His finish, after the move had drawn Roma in and out, was a left-footed chip over the onrushing keeper. There were no signs that the injury would affect his flexibility and spring as he covered every blade of grass at Camp Nou. There he was, breaking the line to latch on to through balls, wriggling away from challenge after challenge, taking a pounding from Roma defenders. Then there was the poacher's goal he scored in the second half, pouncing on an errant finish by Suárez to score at the second attempt. This returning Messi seemed no different from the pre-injury version.

He would score six goals between his comeback and the end of the year. There would also be the small matter of the Ballon d'Or before 2015 ended. The nominations once again contained the names of Messi and Cristiano Ronaldo. The Real Madrid star had outscored Messi during the calendar year, but the Portuguese was under no illusion about who would receive the award. 'I think Messi is going to win this year because this kind of trophy, it depends on votes', Ronaldo told English talk show host Jonathan Ross. The other interesting part of the interview centred on the fact that the pair were on fairly cordial terms.

Ronaldo was right about the winner of the Ballon d'Or. It brought Messi his fifth award, more than any other player. The little man, shunning the garish dinner suits of previous years, dressed simply in traditional evening wear, was as ever, a humble recipient. 'I try to beat my previous self and reach all our goals', said Messi. 'Last year thankfully I managed to reach almost all of them. It was an amazing year that filled us with pride after such good work. It is hard to single out one moment. Our year was full of happiness and victories. It is hard to pick one. These are good players [at Barcelona] with extraordinary quality. We hope that they are going to make us grow. I feel proud of having achieved everything that I have achieved, all my titles. It is always harder to win when you have won before. To come here for the ninth time is truly amazing.'

There had been one more mountain for Messi to conquer before 2015 was out: the final of the Club World Cup, played in Japan. The opponents were River Plate, from Messi's native Argentina, and his penultimate goal of an incredible year was the first of the final. It was a rare, right-footed strike from ten yards with the majority of his body already falling to the floor. He could and should have had more, but Luis Suárez made sure of the 3–0 win with two goals. The Uruguayan would finish the season as top scorer across all the European leagues, the massive investment that had been made in his talents proving to be money well spent.

Barcelona completed their almost annual dispatching of Arsenal in the Champions League. Showing more resolution than normal, Arsenal had blunted Barça for the first hour, before Suárez and Neymar controlled a quick break and Messi calmly beat Petr Čech. A late penalty from the Argentine doubled the score. In the second leg, he withdrew into a deeper role, saving his goal for the closing stages: one of those delicious lobs over the Arsenal goalkeeper. It capped a 3–1 win and a comprehensive 5–1 aggregate victory. Since the Champions League final of 2006, which he missed, Messi had played against Arsenal six times in the competition, and had not been on the losing side.

He continued to score goals in batches of three. His latest hat-trick was against Granada in the Primera División. All three finishes came from inside the penalty area; even in his withdrawn role Messi was able to score archetypal centre-forward goals. Another hat-trick, a month later at home to Valencia, provided a reminder to their new coach, Gary Neville, that The Flea was almost unswattable. Again, all three were scored inside the 18-yard box, Messi benefitting from the movement and delicate footwork of his teammates.

By the start of April 2016, Barcelona had extended their unbeaten run to thirty-nine games. The sequence had started after a defeat at Sevilla in early October. Leo was still recovering from his knee injury at the time, but his return had given Barcelona a freshness. Again, they were fighting on three fronts. In La Liga, they had a sizeable lead over a rejuvenated Real Madrid, now coached by Zinedine Zidane. In the Champions League, they faced a two-legged quarter-final with Atlético Madrid, while a thrashing of Valencia had put them in the final of the Copa del Rey against Sevilla.

One of the aspects about leaving a football legacy is to attempt some kind of skill that will be tried for years to come. Like Pelé's attempted shot from the halfway line at the 1970 World Cup, or the Cruyff Turn four years later. The penalty that Messi produced in the 6–1 victory over Celta Vigo on Valentine's Day 2016, falls into that category. The score was 3–1 with less than ten minutes remaining. Messi's record from the spot was not perfect by any means. As he approached the spot, he slowed his run, as usual. At the moment he would normally strike the ball goalwards, he calmly rolled it to his right, where Suárez ran in and slotted home. The football world was elated, aghast, exasperated and finally full of applause. Thomas Vermaelen, the Barcelona defender, led the positive response when he said: 'I think the players at Camp Nou have always wanted to entertain, and when you are here you feel that way, too. Messi, Suárez and Neymar – they entertain people all around the world, so it's not a bad thing. I don't think it's a lack of respect, it's not like we kick players.' Celta defender Gustavo Cabral said: It's annoying that it ended up being a goal. But not because of the way they took it.'

The MSN were on for another one hundred-goal season and the plaudits they were receiving were fulsome. Barcelona were being compared favourably to all the great teams of yesteryear. They had already broken the Spanish record for most games unbeaten in

They're the three kings – who can take their crowns?

Back to the future

all competitions and were now looking to take the tally to forty. Who stood in their way? Real Madrid. Of course, it had to be. In 1988, Liverpool were on the verge of breaking the unbeaten record in the First Division from the start of a season, previously set by Leeds United. Their opponents in the game that mattered? Everton, their bitter local rivals. In 2004, Arsenal's unbeaten record in the Premier League, which had run since the start of the previous season, was ended by Sir Alex Ferguson's Manchester United, whose domination of English football had been undermined by Arsène Wenger's resurgent side. The fixture list, in all its quirkiness, has a habit of throwing up this type of tantalising match-up at key moments.

On 2 April, on a night full of anticipation and intrigue at Camp Nou, Barcelona took the lead when central defender Gerard Piqué rose to connect with a corner kick in the fifty-sixth minute. Barcelona had been sloppy up to that point, and the much-vaunted MSN were not exempt. Zinedine Zidane's men responded with a superb goal from Karim Benzema, but their fightback seemed to have stalled when Sergio Ramos picked up his customary El Clásico red card. It did not, however, stop Real continuing to press and they were rewarded with the winning goal from the boot of Cristiano Ronaldo. Of course, it had to be.

The end of the unbeaten run started a different sort of sequence. For the next three weeks, from being invincible, Barça seemed keenly aware of their own mortality. They failed to win during that period, and also suffered a Champions League defeat at the hands of Atlético. Perhaps that defeat owed something to fate: since the European Cup had been rebranded, no team had won successive titles. Dreams of another treble were over and their lead at the top of La Liga had been reduced to just a point. It had been as much as ten. The downturn had affected Messi: he had not scored for Barcelona for nearly a month. He finally ended that drought at home against Valencia. But Barça were already 2–0 down and the goal was no more than a consolation. From his understated celebration, it was difficult to grasp the significance of the goal: it was his five-hundredth as a player, 450 of them for Barça. Ronaldo had reached the mark before him, but then he was older and consequently had played at the top level for longer. It was typical of Messi that this individual landmark should only be acknowledged and cherished once Barcelona's slump ended. But for the time being they had both Madrid sides breathing down their neck, and the league title was threatening to slip from their clutches.

Maybe the demands of an incredibly successful but long year were starting to take their toll. There was also the suspicion that when things clicked again, Barcelona would emerge as imperious as ever. When the slump did end, the rebirth was quite stunning. Barça scored twenty-four in the next five league games, with Messi chipping in with three, while the irrepressible Luis Suárez claimed the lion's share with fourteen. They won each game and secured the title, their twenty-fourth and Messi's eighth. The campaign ended with victory in the Copa del Rey, but in keeping with a climax to the season that was filled with tension, there was plenty of drama in the win over Sevilla. It started badly when Javier Mascherano received a straight red card in the early stages. Then Suárez was replaced after sustaining a serious muscle injury. It was a moment for Messi to stand tall. He rose to the occasion and created the two goals in extra time that gave Barça a 2–0 win. First, from the centre of the field, he spotted Jordi Alba making a surging run and found the left-back with unerring accuracy. The defender did the rest. Then, with Sevilla tiring and having committed all their resources in pursuit of an equaliser, Messi slipped a pass for Neymar to score the clinching goal. It was the fourth Copa del Rey title of Messi's career, and in every final he had either scored or created a goal.

After a long, sometimes torturous season, Messi had some injury worries and did not play a full part in the Copa América tournament. However, despite spending chunks of the campaign in the treatment room, he still registered more than forty goals for the eighth successive season. But if he was looking for further motivation, he needed only to look across to the Spanish capital where Real had just won the Champions League for the eleventh time. It was Ronaldo's third chance to hold aloft old Big Ears. Messi had some work to do.

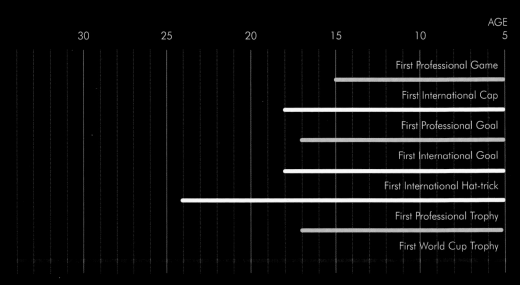

AGE

| 30 | 25 | 20 | 15 | 10 | 5 |

First Professional Game

First International Cap

First Professional Goal

First International Goal

First International Hat-trick

First Professional Trophy

First World Cup Trophy

AGE

| 5 | 10 | 15 | 20 | 25 | 30 |

First Professional Game

First International Cap

First Professional Goal

First International Goal

First International Hat-trick

First Professional Trophy

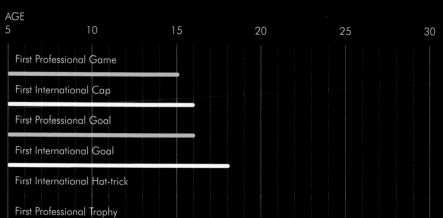

Pelé

Cristiano Ronaldo

Alan Shearer

Wayne Rooney

Lionel Messi

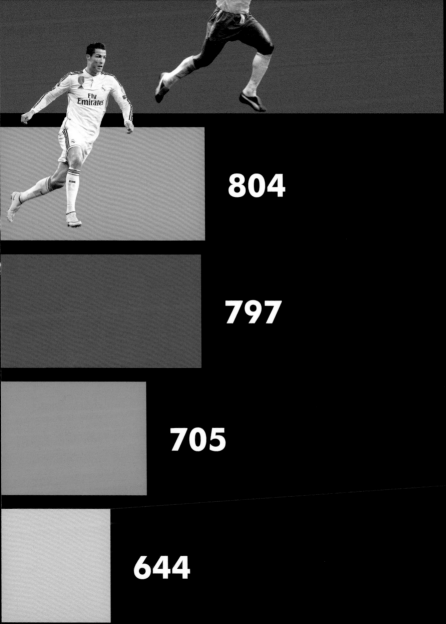

804

797

705

644

12

WHERE TO NOW, YOUNG LEO?

'

I WAS A BIG FAN OF MARADONA GROWING UP AND OF THE CURRENT CROP RONALDO IS GOOD BUT MESSI IS THE BEST I'VE EVER SEEN. I DON'T DISH OUT PRAISE LIGHTLY BUT MESSI DESERVES IT. I LOOK FOR WEAKNESSES IN HIS GAME AND I CAN'T FIND THEM.

'

Roy Keane

In pre-season training for the 2016–17 season, Lionel Messi returned looking quite different. The evolution from boy to man had taken place long ago, and the puppy fat that used to shape his features had disappeared with it. The longish hair had also become a thing of the past. But while the hair might be shorter, now suddenly it was blond. He was back on the training ground, doing drills with his Barcelona teammates, but it was clear that his new style had given his colleagues a giggle.

Already one of those teammates, Luis Suárez, had hinted that Leo's international retirement might be short-lived. Suárez was one of the players who could benefit from Messi's decision to say goodbye to the national team, not least because Uruguay were one of Argentina's regular rivals at the Copa América. But football at the highest level needs its great players and Suárez knew that. There were two years until the next World Cup and it seemed unthinkable that Messi, who would then be approaching his thirty-first birthday, would not be there.

As Messi approaches the twilight of his career, there will come a day when he will not be Barcelona's main man. Maybe not immediately, but soon enough. The zip, the acceleration, the stamina will start to disappear and he will have to rely on his vast array of tricks. There were hints during the 2015–16 season, especially in the Copa del Rey final, that the role of midfield playmaker may be the future for a more mature Messi. He shares the same year of birth as Suárez and it is possible that both will tail off at the same time. However, Suárez remains a striker to his core so his reinvention is harder to foresee. The other member of the MSN, the Brazilian Neymar, may then become the key man at Barcelona. Certainly, that was the view of Alessandro Del Piero, the legendary former Juventus and Italy player. He told Brazilian television in summer 2016 that Neymar was the 'leader of the future'. At five years Messi's junior, Neymar is likely to outstay the Argentine at Camp Nou, but his ascendancy to Messi's throne is some way off. Despite being in the Barcelona first team for more than a decade, Messi still wants to play every game and despises being substituted. There will come a time when he appreciates the rest, but for now that is only countenanced because of injury.

HIGHEST NUMBER OF CAREER GOALS

Up until the end of the 2015–16 season.

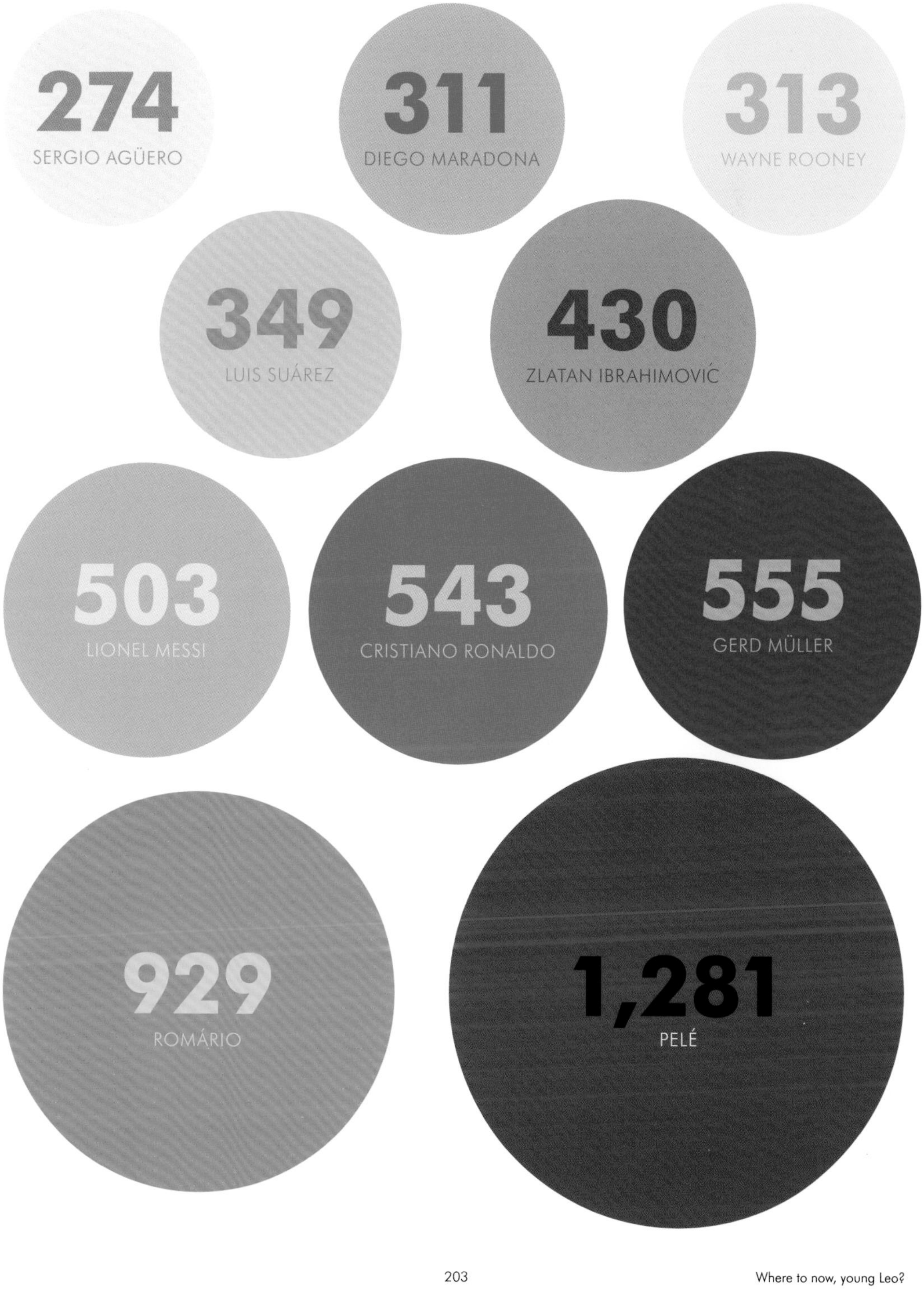

274
SERGIO AGÜERO

311
DIEGO MARADONA

313
WAYNE ROONEY

349
LUIS SUÁREZ

430
ZLATAN IBRAHIMOVIĆ

503
LIONEL MESSI

543
CRISTIANO RONALDO

555
GERD MÜLLER

929
ROMÁRIO

1,281
PELÉ

Where to now, young Leo?

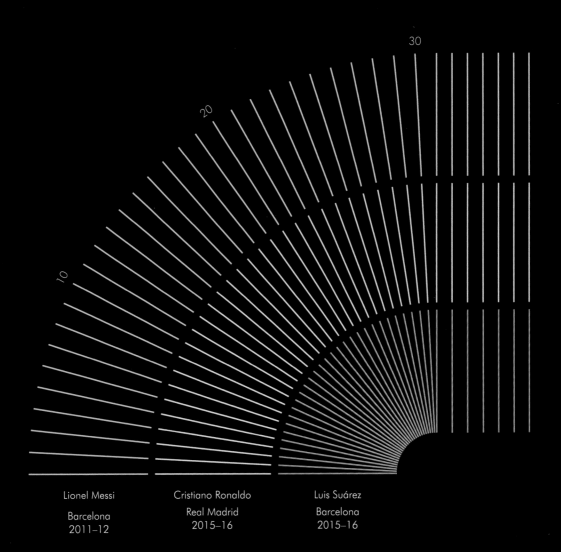

30

20

10

Lionel Messi

Barcelona
2011–12

Cristiano Ronaldo

Real Madrid
2015–16

Luis Suárez

Barcelona
2015–16

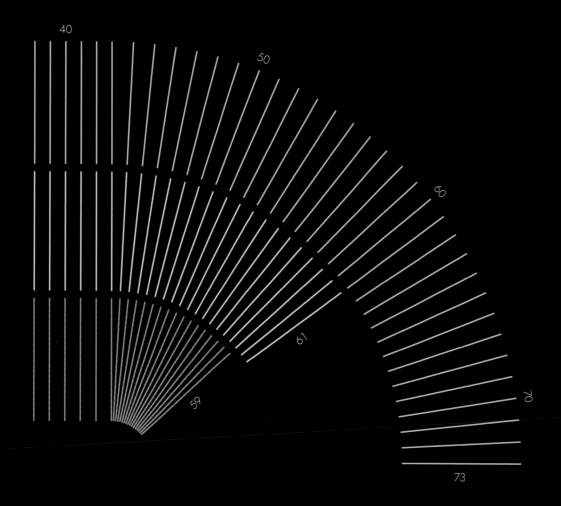

Where to now, young Leo?

Indeed, early in 2016, Messi said: 'I feel very good physically and mentally. I am having so much fun every time I go out on the pitch. I've always said I am happy in Barcelona and as long as the club and the people want, I'll be happy to help them face new challenges. If injuries respect me, and I still have some luck, my intention is to play for many more years.'

That sense of fun was clear when he played with Suárez and Neymar. The trio seemed to have the same desire to play a brand of innovative football. The flips, the spins and the goals. Messi enjoyed all that, but it was the victories that mattered most, and the competition. It will be interesting to see how Messi responds if and when his rival and nemesis Cristiano Ronaldo starts to exhibit true signs of weakness. What seemed clear as the 2016–17 season kicked off was that Messi was still in love with football, just as he was when he first kicked a ball as a kid. And what we call his need for reinvention might be no more than evolution.

Messi has already become Barcelona's leading all-time goalscorer and the top scorer in the history of La Liga. If there are other targets, they are probably in taking his tally to six hundred goals, and then maybe past the seven-hundred mark. He has scored at a rate in excess of forty goals a season for the best part of a decade, so they are not outrageous targets.

It is impossible to say where his future lies after football, though. One day he will return to his native Argentina and enjoy more privacy than he does in Europe. It is hard to see him becoming a coach or a manager. The truly great players often avoid a life in coaching, the obvious exception being Johan Cruyff. But the Dutchman was always governed by strong principles about how the game should be played and what made it beautiful. So much of his management ethos was just an extension of his personality. In an age where everyone has the ability to voice an opinion, and for it to be heard, not always for the best, Leo's voice is surprisingly quiet and seldom heard. He may agree with every word said by Cruyff, but his true feelings have never been made public.

However, his insistence that Suárez should take over his favoured central striking position shows that Messi does have football opinions and sees the game above and beyond his own personal gain. The fact that he has managed to subsequently reinvent himself, and maintain his frightening goal output, suggests someone with a superior football brain. It also underlines that when his athletic powers start to wane, Messi is likely to have a solution to combat it. After all, his pace and power have only been part of what makes him a truly special player; it is his vision and the ability to bring players into the game that enhance his profile.

When he finally walks away from the game he loves so much, the only question is whether he will have a World Cup victory on his *curriculum vitae*. It is the one major trophy missing from his cabinet. Having coped with the pressure of being the world's best player for nearly a decade, little Leo must be contemplating one last tilt at the tournament that unites all Argentines in Russia in 2018. Then his legacy will be complete.

Planning a life away from international football can wait for a few more years.

MOST GOALS EVER SCORED IN A CALENDAR YEAR

Lionel Messi, 2012

04 Jan	Osasuna	Copa Del rey	2	4–0
15 Jan	Real Betis	La Liga	2	4–2
22 Jan	Málaga	La Liga	3	4–1
04 Feb	R.Sociedad	La Liga	1	2–1
14 Feb	B.Leverkusen	CL- 2.round	1	3–1
19 Feb	Valencia	La Liga	4	5–1
26 Feb	A.Madrid	La Liga	1	2–1
29 Feb	Switzerland	Int. Friendly	3	3–1
07 Mar	B.Leverkusen	CL- 2.round	5	7–1
11 Mar	R.Santander	La Liga	2	2–0
17 Mar	Sevilla	La Liga	1	2–0
20 Mar	Granada	La Liga	3	5–3
24 Mar	Mallorca	La Liga	1	2–0
31 Mar	A.Bilbao	La Liga	1	2–0
03 Apr	AC Milan	CL- Quarter final	2	3–1
07 Apr	R.Zaragoza	La Liga	2	4–1
10 Apr	Getafe	La Liga	1	4–0
14 Apr	Levante	La Liga	2	2–1
29 Apr	R.Vallecano	La Liga	2	7–0
02 May	Málaga	La Liga	3	4–1
05 May	Espanyol	La Liga	4	4–0
25 May	A. Bilbao	Copa del Rey final	1	3–0
03 Jun	Ecuador	WC-Qualif.	1	4–0
09 Jun	Brazil	Int. Friendly	3	4–3

15 Aug	Germany	Int. Friendly	1	4–3
19 Aug	R.Sociedad	La Liga	2	5–1
23 Aug	Real Madrid	Spanish Super Cup	1	3–2
26 Aug	Osasuna	La Liga	2	2–1
29 Aug	Real Madrid	Spanish Super Cup	1	1–2
07 Sep	Paraguay	WC-Qualif.	1	3–1
15 Sep	Getafe	La Liga	2	4–1
19 Sep	Sp.Moscow	CL Group st.	2	3–2
07 Oct	Real Madrid	La Liga	2	2–2
12 Oct	Uruguay	WC-Qualif.	2	3–0
16 Oct	Chile	WC-Qualif.	1	2–1
20 Oct	Dep Cor	La Liga	3	5–4
27 Oct	Rayo Vallec.	La Liga	2	5–0
07 Nov	Celtic	CL Group st.	1	1–2
11 Nov	Mallorca	La Liga	2	4–2
17 Nov	Real Zaragoza	La Liga	2	3–1
20 Nov	Sp.Moscow	CL Group st.	2	3–0
25 Nov	Levante	La Liga	2	4–0
01 Dec	Athletic Bilbao	La Liga	2	5–1
09 Dec	Real Betis	La Liga	2	2–1
12 Dec	Cordoba	Copa del Rey	2	2–0
16 Dec	At.Madrid	La Liga	2	4–1
22 Dec	R.Valladolid	La Liga	1	3–1

● 1 Goal   ● 2 Goals ● 3 Goals ● 4 Goals ● 5 Goals

Where to now, young Leo?

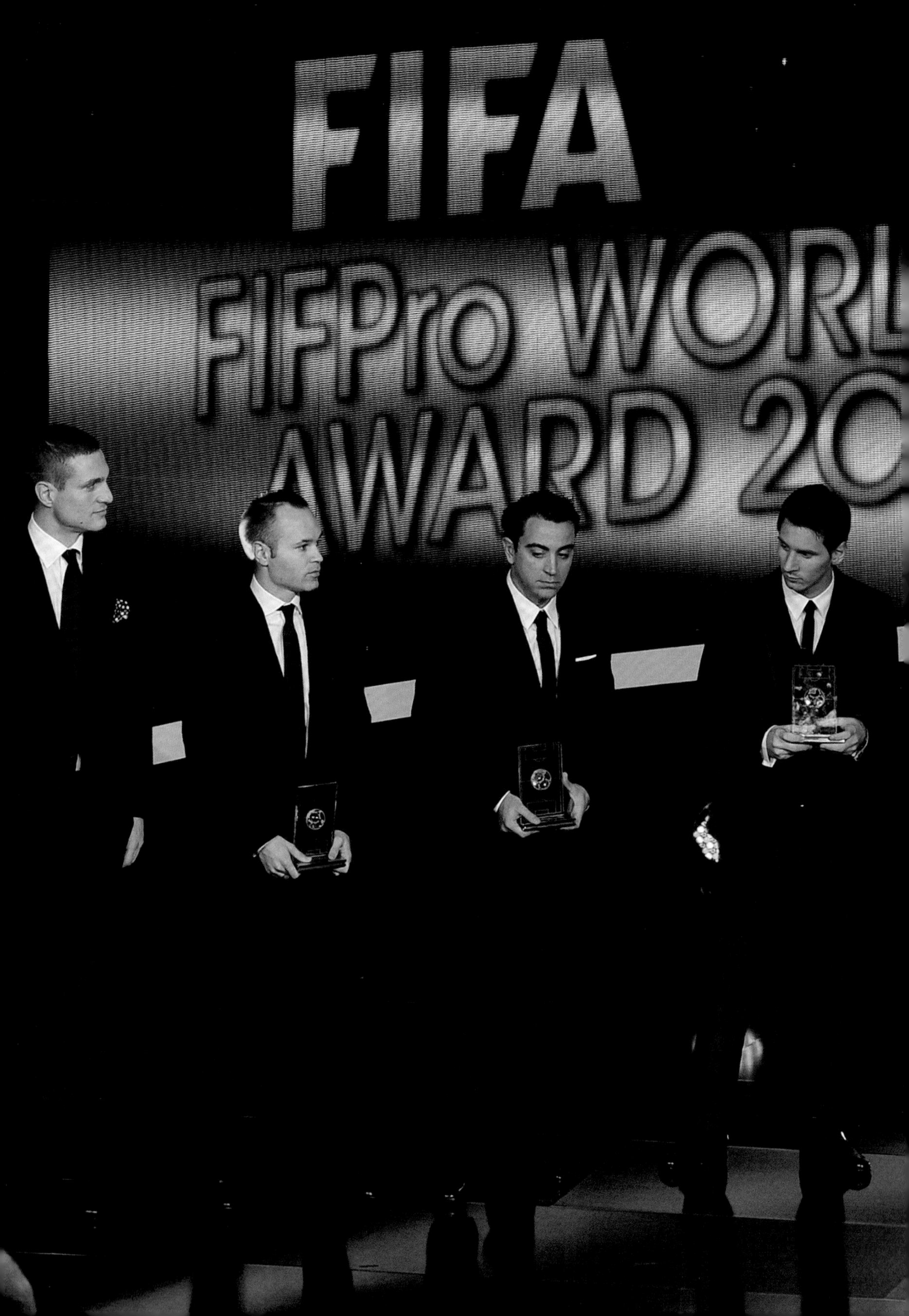
FIFA
FIFPro WORL
AWARD 20

13

TAKE YOUR PLACE, LEO – BUT WHERE DO YOU SIT?

'

FELLA'S A GENIUS. BEST EVER BY A DISTANCE IN MY LIFETIME. NEVER REALLY SAW PELÉ... SOUNESS, GULLIT, VENABLES AND NOW ROONEY AGREE MESSI IS THE BEST THEY HAVE SEEN. HE PLAYS A GAME WITH WHICH WE ARE NOT FAMILIAR.

'

Gary Lineker

When asked a few years ago who was the best player in the world, the venerable Arsenal manager Arsène Wenger was unequivocal. 'Lionel Messi', he said. When asked who was the best ever, his answer was the same. Gary Lineker, the former England and Barcelona striker, now a successful television presenter, says we should not even 'argue the point'. Messi's former teammate Ronaldinho knew how good he was going to be after their first training session together. In terms of what others think of him, Messi is keeping company with the best in football's Pantheon. But football has a rich and wonderful history, so it is worth investigating who came before him before making a definitive assessment.

Before Messi, there was... Zinedine Zidane. He was a totally different footballer who played across the midfield and seemed to defy his muscular stature by producing consistently skilful performances. He carried teams to glory on his back, such was the force of his personality. Nowhere was that better illustrated than when France won the World Cup in 1998 and the European Championship two years later. His club honours were no less impressive: he helped Juventus to successive league titles in the late 1990s, and Real Madrid to the Champions League title in 2002. His winning goal against Bayer Leverkusen was perhaps the finest seen in a European final.

Zidane was FIFA World Player of the Year three times, as well as the Ballon d'Or winner in 1998, and his trophy cabinet bulged with any number of other awards as befitted a player of his ability. And yet. This was also a player with a serious temperamental flaw: he was sent off fourteen times in his career, most notably in the 2006 World Cup final for a butt on the Italian defender Marco Materazzi. France lost that game and Zidane would offer no excuses for his conduct, except that he was provoked. It is mere conjecture whether his continued presence on the field would have changed the outcome of the match, suffice it to say the contest was decided by a penalty shoot-out. As Zidane had already scored from the spot, he would certainly have been one of France's first five takers.

Just as Zidane's career was starting, so that of Diego Maradona was drawing to a close. Speed, balance and skill were Diego's trademarks. He could also take the physical pounding frequently dished out by defenders who operated in a less civilised and patrolled football world. His contribution towards Argentina success in the 1986 World Cup cannot be underplayed, though he will always be tainted by the 'Hand of God' goal in the quarter-final against England. But a much truer reflection of his talents came a short while later in the same game when he beat half the England team on the way to scoring a goal considered by many as the greatest ever scored. He is also fondly remembered by Napoli supporters for taking the Italian side to two Serie A titles, and at Barcelona where he won three major honours in 1983. In contrast to Messi, he is revered in Argentina because he began his professional career at home, playing for Boca Juniors, before moving to Europe for a record fee. The fact he also returned after his European glory days had ended, when his body was clearly in pain, added to his reputation.

But Maradona's fame came at a cost: there was an addiction to drugs that dated from the mid-1980s followed by the dramatic decline in his health which almost cost him his life in 2004. His fondness for alcohol saw him seek rehabilitation. The problems he had to deal with are in keeping with someone who came to a new country and continent at an impressionable age, without the kind of support that footballers enjoy nowadays. In his pomp Maradona had to live with the tag of being the best footballer in the world; he had no realistic challengers. Messi, on the other hand, has had the constant battle with Cristiano Ronaldo to keep him on his toes. Maradona has a personality that remains utterly vibrant. There are similarities to another legend, Muhammad Ali, who was as reviled as he was revered during the height of his sporting brilliance.

Going back chronologically, the man with whom Maradona is most often compared is Pelé. The Brazilian is the only man to win three World Cups, and one of the few to score more than one thousand goals. Forget the current incarnation of Pelé, with a Subway-

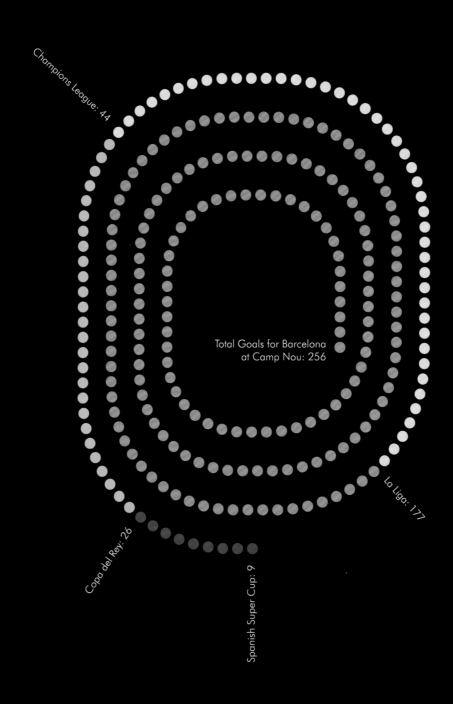

Champions League: 44

La Liga: 177

Copa del Rey: 26

Spanish Super Cup: 9

Total Goals for Barcelona
at Camp Nou: 256

PERSONAL TROPHIES

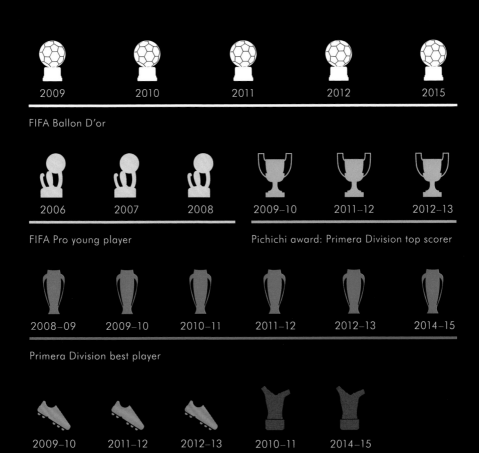

| 2009 | 2010 | 2011 | 2012 | 2015 |

FIFA Ballon D'or

| 2006 | 2007 | 2008 | 2009–10 | 2011–12 | 2012–13 |

FIFA Pro young player

Pichichi award: Primera Division top scorer

| 2008–09 | 2009–10 | 2010–11 | 2011–12 | 2012–13 | 2014–15 |

Primera Division best player

| 2009–10 | 2011–12 | 2012–13 | 2010–11 | 2014–15 |

European Golden Shoe

UEFA best player

2014/15

UEFA best goal vs Bayern Munich,
Champions League, second goal.

Take your place, Leo – but where do you sit?

adorned T-shirt, and various other brands using him as an advertising mannequin, and salute instead the player who was literally kicked out of tournaments because he was so good. Pelé's notable quality, one that draws Messi closer to him, is that his greatness could flourish around others of similar standing. In 1958, when he won his first World Cup, he and Garrincha stood out as Brazil's best players. In 1970, when he was a member of arguably the greatest international side in history, Jairzinho, Tostão, Gérson, Carlos Alberto and Rivelino would all be contenders alongside him for an all-time best XI. Similarly, Messi has stood above such contemporaries as Andrés Iniesta, Xavi, David Villa and recently Luis Suárez and Neymar.

Pelé and Maradona played in an era when the flair players did not receive the protection from referees that the modern player does. But both had careers that started when they were teenagers and carried on well into their late thirties. Both played in forward positions, but were happy to take the ball deep and create havoc from there. There can only be speculation about how Pelé and Maradona would have fared in the modern era with new training methods and greater awareness of the importance of a healthy diet. Messi is playing at as high a level as both of them, and in an era where football is more sophisticated. At the highest level, most players watch videos of their opponents and also receive tips on how to combat their strengths and exploit their weaknesses. It is like Championship Manager but with reality added. That is the world in which Messi operates, and he does so without weakness or complaint. Whereas injury, caused by repeated punishment by his opponents, undoubtedly hampered the latter stages of Maradona's career, Messi has altered the way he plays. He is less willing to engage in physical battles with his opponents and instead picks up the ball in areas of less danger to himself.

Where Messi cannot compete – yet – is with Pelé and Maradona's international achievements. He has been dogged by misfortune when he has been close to getting his hands on the World Cup: in 2010, Maradona was his coach and his lack of experience quickly became apparent; in 2014, Argentina were only beaten by a German side who may go down as one of the best sides in history. There may be time for him to rectify that omission, but in every other aspect Messi has proved he is at the very least their equal. The wide range of goals he has scored, from distance, dribbles, close range, headers, volleys, as well as the goals he has made, showcase his talent. Once he was young and precocious. Then he was Barça's main man. Now he has become the side's elder statesman, and is, perhaps, even more influential.

MESSI VS RONALDO AS CAPTAIN

Messi	
Club Captain	n/a
Titles Won as Captain	Spanish Super Cup
	Captain was injured, Messi was vice-captain
Captain of National Team	Since August 2011
Titles Won as Captain	3 consecutive finals of 2014 World Cup,
	and the 2015 and 2016 Copas America.

Ronaldo	
Club Captain	Since September 2016
Titles Won as Captain	—
Captain of National Team	6 February 2007 – 10 October 2016
Titles Won as Captain	European Champion 2016

PREDICTED GOALS IF MESSI CONTINUES TO 35

A look at how many goals Messi will score if he continues his incredible rate up to the age of thirty-five.

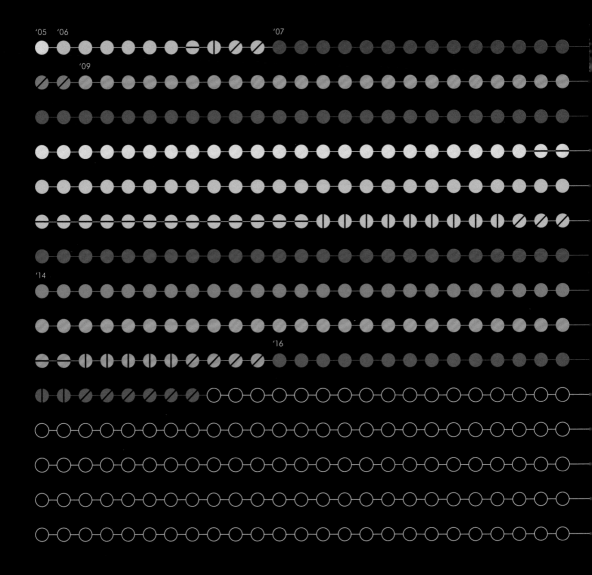

'05 '06 '07 '09 '14 '16

● League Goals   ◖ Other Cup Competitions   ○ Predictions

◒ Champions League   ◪ Internationals

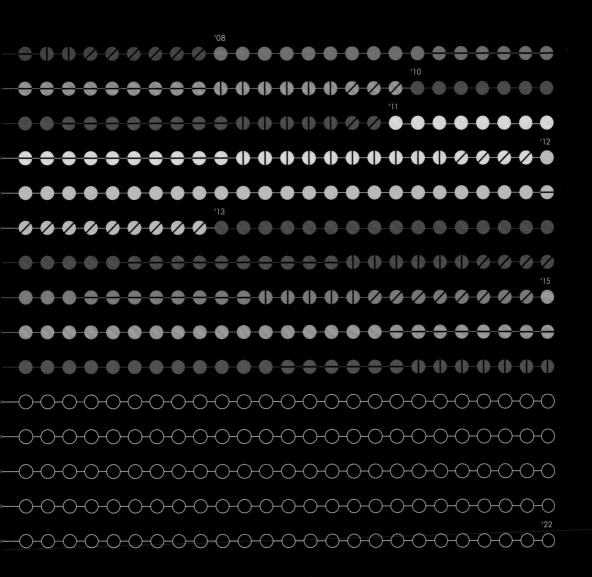

Take your place, Leo — but where do you sit?

BEING MESSI BRINGS ITS OWN REWARDS

14

‘

I WEAR THE NUMBER 10 JERSEY FOR THE US NATIONAL TEAM IN HONOUR OF THE GREATEST ATHLETE I HAVE EVER SEEN: MESSI.

Kobe Bryant

PLAYER SALARIES

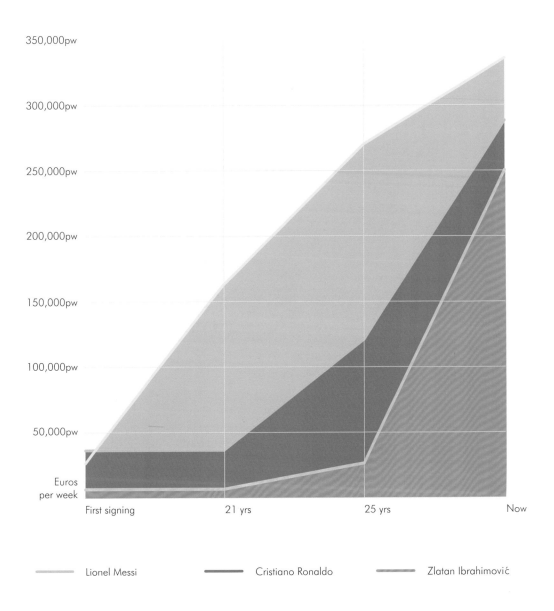

350,000pw

300,000pw

250,000pw

200,000pw

150,000pw

100,000pw

50,000pw

Euros
per week

First signing   21 yrs   25 yrs   Now

———— Lionel Messi   ———— Cristiano Ronaldo   ———— Zlatan Ibrahimović

Lionel Messi's first 'wage' was in the shape of extra ice creams for doing keepy-uppys back home in Rosario. When he signed his first contract at Barcelona at the age of sixteen he received a more than livable fifteen hundred euros a week. There were performance-related clauses including an increase when he made his first-team debut. The moment he played in that first friendly match, the figure rose to ten thousand euros a week. Before that, the club had provided accommodation for him and his family as well as paying his medical bills.

By June 2005, after he had scored his first professional goal, he was put on a five-year deal that paid him twenty-five thousand euros a week. Remarkably, that deal was renegotiated three months later, and the figure doubled. In an era where young talent was craved and bought at a high price, he was the highest paid teenager in football. In March 2007, having scored his first hat-trick for Barcelona, he signed another deal paying one hundred thousand euros a week. Just a year later, having doubled his salary again, he signed a contract that made him the highest paid player at the club at the age of twenty-one.

Only a year later, on the back of winning three trophies, and having scored in the Champions League final, the Argentine agreed yet another contract. It was for seven years and paid him one million euros every four weeks. It made him the highest paid footballer on Earth. He has since agreed two more contract extensions, the latter paying him an unprecedented four hundred thousand euros a week after tax. The deal's length is unknown but it runs at least until 2018. At the moment, Barcelona's investment is estimated to be around 479 million euros. Messi has a buyout clause, standard practice in Spanish football, of 250 million euros.

At the start of 2016, Lionel Messi's personal wealth was put at 316 million euros. He has a lucrative contract with Adidas, which pays him nearly twenty million euros a year, and other brand deals mean he is the second highest paid athlete in the world. Guess who is number one? The answer is his chief rival, Cristiano Ronaldo. Behind Messi are the likes of basketball player LeBron James, tennis player Roger Federer and golfer Tiger Woods. These lucrative deals have enabled Messi to start his own foundation to help young children who are being denied

EARNINGS IN COMPARISON TO OTHER SPORTSMEN

The highest earning sportsmen of 2016.

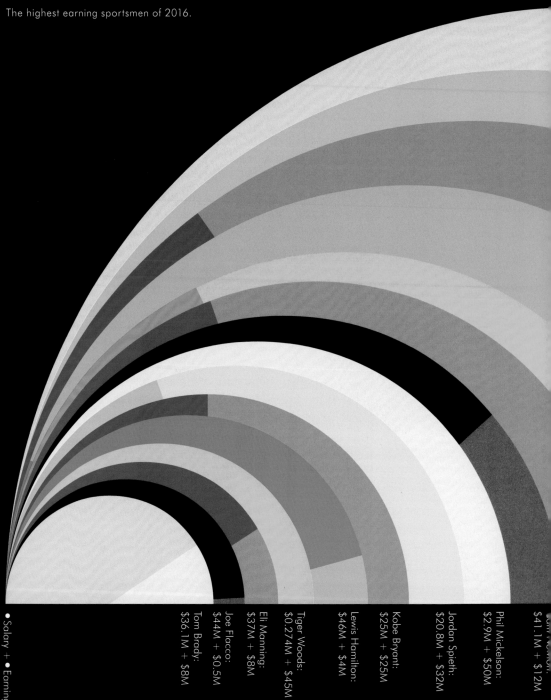

● Salary + ● Earnings

$41.1M + $12M

Phil Mickelson:
$2.9M + $50M

Jordan Spieth:
$20.8M + $32M

Kobe Bryant:
$25M + $25M

Lewis Hamilton:
$46M + $4M

Tiger Woods:
$0.274M + $45M

Eli Manning:
$37M + $8M

Joe Flacco:
$44M + $0.5M

Tom Brady:
$36.1M + $8M

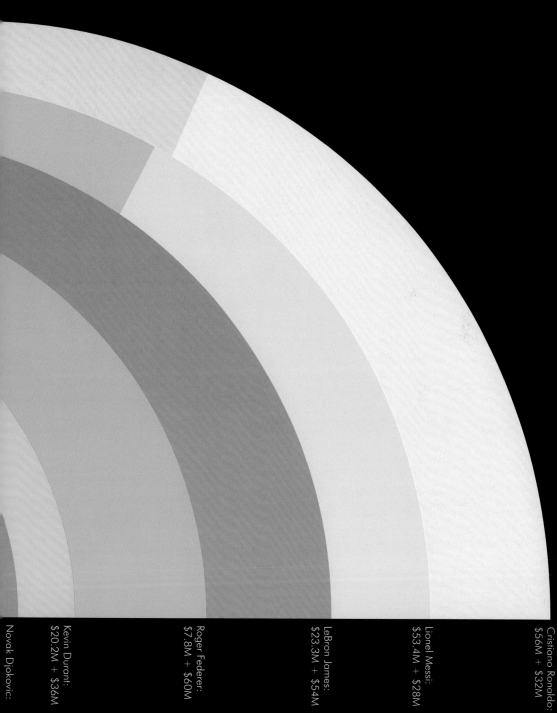

Cristiano Ronaldo:
$56M + $32M

Lionel Messi:
$53.4M + $28M

LeBron James:
$23.3M + $54M

Roger Federer:
$7.8M + $60M

Kevin Durant:
$20.2M + $36M

Novak Djokovic:

Being Messi brings its own rewards

access to education, health care and sports. He is also an ambassador for Unicef and has made sizable donations over the years, none bigger than the one he made in 2015: the organisation announced on Twitter that the footballer had donated 4.5 million Argentine pesos, the equivalent of around 260,000 euros.

Although he remains an intensely private person, rarely seen at celebrity events, Messi does enjoy the trappings that go with being a wealthy footballer. He lives in a house worth nearly five million euros in the Castelldefels area of Barcelona, and reportedly bought out his neighbours in 2013 because they made too much noise. He has the footballer's obligatory fleet of cars, including a white Maserati and a Ferrari. He also has an impressive collection of tattoos. He has one on the left side of his back, which is a portrait of his mother. There are two tattoos on his left calf, one a copy of his eldest son's hand print, the other a football-themed piece of ink which contains his number ten. Finally there is the sleeve tattoo which was only revealed when it peeped out from under his shirt a few years ago, and which has religious themes.

Messi has two sons. Thiago was born on 2 November 2012 and he was joined by Mateo on 11 September 2015. Both the children are a result of a relationship he has had since 2008 with Antonella Roccuzzo, who he has known since the age of five.

On the negative side, in 2016 Messi was found guilty of tax fraud by a Spanish court and received a twenty-one-month prison sentence – which under Spanish law can be served on probation – and ordered to pay a fine reported to be 1.7 million euros. He had been charged with setting up a string of fake companies in Belize and Uruguay to avoid paying tax on 4.16 million euros of image-rights earnings between 2007 and 2009. During the trial, Messi did little to alter the picture that had been created of him as a football-mad boy who left his financial affairs to his father and who never looked at the contracts he signed. At the time Messi said he planned to appeal the verdict.

As far as endorsements go, Messi has been the face of both the long-running video games *FIFA* and *Pro Evolution Soccer*. When he is not playing football or looking after his two children, legend has it that he still has a child-like enthusiasm for the computer games. Lionel Messi will be thirty in 2017, and while this is a young man who just happens to be the best footballer alive, he is very much a boy at heart. Within seventy-two hours of the birth of his eldest son, he had signed him up for Newell's Old Boys, the club where it is expected he will finish his career. By that stage, there will not be any more records for young Leo to break.

No really, I just have two feet like you. One of Messi's fans runs onto the pitch to express his awe at Messi's incredible talent.

Being Messi brings its own rewards

EARNINGS IN COMPARISON TO CELEBRITIES

The highest earning celebrities of 2016.

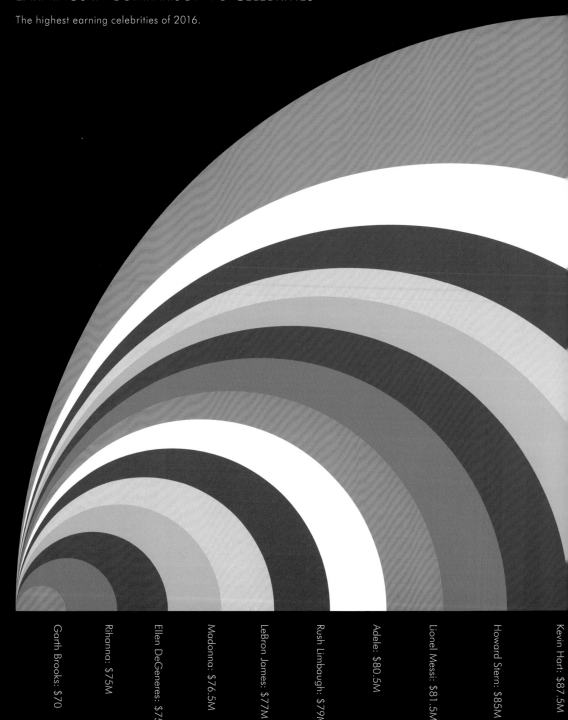

Garth Brooks: $70

Rihanna: $75M

Ellen DeGeneres: $75M

Madonna: $76.5M

LeBron James: $77M

Rush Limbaugh: $79M

Adele: $80.5M

Lionel Messi: $81.5M

Howard Stern: $85M

Kevin Hart: $87.5M

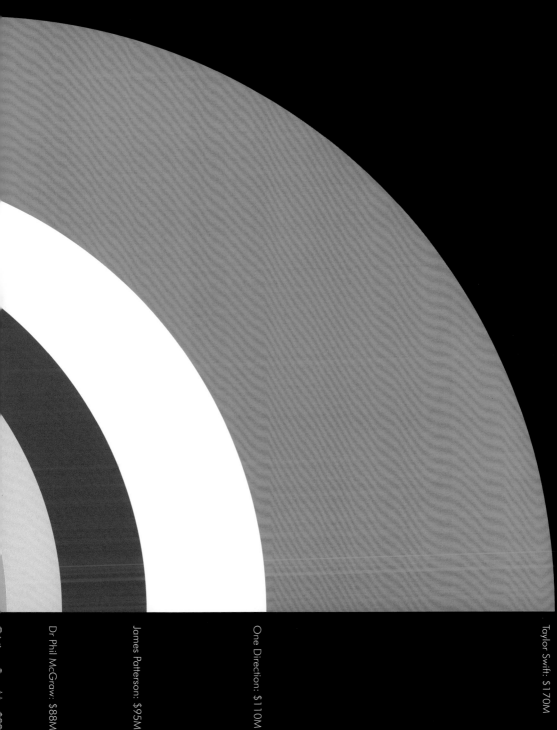

Taylor Swift: $170M

One Direction: $110M

James Patterson: $95M

Dr Phil McGraw: $88M

Being Messi brings its own rewards

15

BEHIND EVERY GREAT MAN

'

MESSI IS GOD, AS A PERSON AND EVEN MORE AS A PLAYER. I KNEW HIM WHEN HE WAS A BOY AND I'VE WATCHED HIM GROW. HE DESERVES IT ALL.

,

Samuel Eto'o

Back in 2006, Rafael Benítez was looking to improve on the Liverpool squad who had just won the FA Cup, a season after their unbelievable Champions League victory over AC Milan. The Merseyside club had just finished their Premier League campaign in an impressive third position, nine points behind champions Chelsea. Benítez had already identified the player he knew would improve a side that already included Steven Gerrard, Xabi Alonso and Jamie Carragher. The player he wanted was largely unknown to British football fans, a Brazilian right-back at Sevilla who could also play on the right wing. Benítez had been mocked for his fondness of the Spanish market, but he was convinced this player was the real deal. He had done his homework about the player, his life away from the pitch and his dedication to the game. Liverpool failed to agree a deal with the player, or more importantly, the club's president José María del Nido. Two years later, the player in question, Dani Alves, joined Barcelona for thirty million euros.

When Lionel Messi reached five hundred career goals during the 2015–16 season, the statistics provided some interesting reading. Analysing his goals, it was no surprise to see that Andrés Iniesta and Xavi were prominent in the list of those who had provided the scoring opportunity for many of them. What was surprising was that Dani Alves led the way with forty-two assists for Messi during his eight years at the club. It did not, however, surprise the two people who matter most: the man who signed him and the man who had benefited. Pep Guardiola said at the time: 'His signing is very good news for the club. Along with Messi, if they work together, we will have the best right flank in the world.' The coach's dream became reality to the extent that in 2015, when it became clear that Alves was about to start his final season at Camp Nou, Messi said: 'Alves is the best full-back in the world. It is very difficult to find a player like him.'

Iniesta and Xavi were joint second on the list of Messi providers. Before the 2011 Champions League final, Manchester United manager Sir Alex Ferguson had said that the 'passing carousel' the pair weaved along with Messi would unhinge any side who let them take charge. Xavi was particularly effusive about his long-time midfield compadre,

Iniesta. 'He's the most talented Spanish player of all time', he said. 'He's excellent at everything, such as the way he treats people, and he is an example in the dressing room and on the pitch. He's a leader. He always wants the ball, he never hides. That isn't easy to find [in players]. Aside from his talent, he makes a difference in all areas of the pitch. He's extraordinary. It's an absolute pleasure to have spent so many years playing alongside him.'

The appreciation was mutual. Iniesta reciprocated by saying: 'If I start speaking about Xavi, I really do not know where to start. It was a privilege to play alongside him – throughout my playing years in the club and the national team. We'd be sure about each other's position on the ground without even looking at each other.'

Both players played crucial roles in Barcelona's success, but both recognised that their jobs had been made a whole lot easier by the boy from Rosario. 'For us he's the number one whether he scores or not', said Iniesta of Messi. Xavi chipped in: 'He's the smallest, but he's the best at everything, even in the air.'

The passing carousel was not unique to Barcelona, but has become very much associated with them. Pep Guardiola and Luis Enrique, the foremost coaches during Messi's time at the club, were chiefly responsible for making the carousel work. Messi and Guardiola are not that close now that they do not work together. But few relationships have been as fruitful as theirs in such a comparatively short period of time. It is said that in their first conversation when Guardiola took over as coach, he told the then twenty-year-old Messi that he would make him a thirty-goal-a-season striker. By the end of their first campaign, the Argentine had beaten that target, outshining illustrious teammates like Samuel Eto'o and Thierry Henry. In the four seasons that Messi was coached by Guardiola, his goal tally improved.

One of Guardiola's most greatly admired assets is his work ethic. The former midfield playmaker, who was part of Johan Cruyff's 'Dream Team' of the early 1990s, is known to work fifteen-hour days to prepare his sides and make them better. It has clearly paid off given that Barcelona and then Bayern Munich won six out of a seven possible league titles during his time in charge. He is a perfectionist at work, and a lot of that influence comes from his time playing under Cruyff. It is also instructive that since Guardiola retired from playing he has taken two year-long sabbaticals. That time away has shaped and sometimes changed his philosophy of football.

Guardiola's football is largely possession-based, but he is keen that his team should be ready to press when the opposition have the ball in order to regain it. It was not unusual for his sides to have nearly seventy per cent possession of the ball during the ninety minutes. That benefits someone like Messi, who does not enjoy himself if he is having to chase around. Guardiola created the 'false number nine' position for Messi to stop teams laying siege to Barcelona's right wing and marking the young man out of the game.

The coach himself says: 'People talk about tactics, but when you look at it, tactics are just players. You change things so that the team can get the most out of the skills they have to offer, but you don't go any further than that. When it comes to tactics you have to think about what the opposition does and the players who can hurt you. What I've done is a response to the game-plans our rivals are now adopting against us. As time goes by, people get to know you better. They pose problems for you and you have to come up with solutions.'

There has been much speculation about the fact that Luis Enrique and Messi do not enjoy the same bond as other coaches and players. There were certainly problems at the start of their relationship. But whereas Messi enjoys the status of being the best player in the world, Enrique's mandate when he moved up from Barcelona B to the A team was to restore the side to the heights of the Guardiola period. The side had treaded water for two seasons, and needed to move in a slightly different direction. The dream forward three of Messi, Suárez and Neymar, the MSN, had not been integrated in such a way that they were able to produce performances commensurate with their talents. The solution seemed to come when Messi suggested that he swap positions with Suárez and take back his old right-wing berth. Certainly the weight on his back was eased by the arrival of Suárez

108

APPEARANCES

8

TROPHIES

100

GOALS

52

ASSISTS

2014–15

2014–15

2014–15

2015

2015

2015–16

2015–16

2016

 Copa del Rey

 UEFA Champions League

 FIFA Club World Cup

 La Liga

 Spanish Super Cup

 UEFA Super Cup

Behind every great man

Messi and Luis Enrique have not shown the same close relationship
that Leo shared with Pep, but their results speak for themselves.

and Neymar. Their tireless running reinvigorated him at a time in his career when he might have had doubts about the direction in which he was heading.

Enrique's philosophy seems less fixed than Guardiola's. The main thing he has changed is the speed with which asks his players to move the ball. It is designed to make the most of the explosive nature of Suárez and Neymar. The fact that Enrique allowed the move to take place, and through other subtle changes make the team flourish, has shown him to be the definition of the modern coach. Barcelona now is closer to the image of him as a player: possession-based but with an accent on strong running.

Enrique's methods show that while he may never have the relationship with Messi that the Argentine shared with Guardiola, he may be the coach the player needs at this stage of his career: the manager he may not like to spend time with but the one who gets the most out of him. There was little doubt that in the season before Enrique's arrival, Messi had lost a little love for his own position at the club. Speaking at the end of the 2014–15 season, Messi had said: 'I think it was a bit tough to begin with. It's always hard to change things. But once we started doing what we wanted to do, what the coach wanted to do, we gradually began to improve and perform better and better. Fortunately, we had a great year.'

Enrique is a man of fewer words, rarely giving interviews to journalists outside his contractual obligations around a match. But before the Champions League fixture against Arsenal in the 2015–16 season, he was moved to discuss the Messi he was working with and the player he was seeing evolving in front of him. The coach said: 'Last season he was unbelievable, he did pretty much everything: he scored goals, he made defensive sacrifices and assists. This season he is at the same level, or even higher. My players are capable of reinventing themselves constantly. Whenever Lionel Messi goes back into midfield he becomes the best midfielder. Now he plays on the wing, but has the freedom to create superiority in certain areas of the pitch and he is our leader.'

It is a given that when a player represents Barcelona, to make himself more popular he has to do his best against local rivals Espanyol and historical rivals Real Madrid. There is a growing chasm between the abilities and achievements of the two sides based in Catalonia. But the rivalry between Barça and Real has never been greater. If you are good enough to score a goal against Real, the likelihood is that you will receive a free drink or meal in a Barça bar for life. Messi has scored twenty-one goals against *Los Blancos*, with thirteen assists. The first time he scored against them, it was a hat-trick. He is the only player to have scored two hat-tricks against them and he has won nearly twice as many times as he has lost to Real. He also understands the rivalry, despite being a boy from Rosario. Maybe it was because he spent so much time at La Masia with boys raised in the area. Certainly, there are quotes attributed to him about his preference for an Atlético win in the all-Madrid Champions League final of 2016. Messi would still be great if he had never scored against Real, but the fact he is so prolific against them has only enhanced his legend.

Real covet him as well. There is general acceptance that they have tried to sign him on several occasions in the past decade. On 1 April 2016 a paper ran a spoof story which claimed he had made the switch to the Bernabéu. Reshmin Chowdhury, now a reporter for BT Sport, spent two years at Real Madrid TV as Messi was coming through the ranks. She remembers that he was 'annoyingly good'. She said: 'He was an incredible talent. He was just a whizzkid, this small player with incredible feet. And as someone who followed Real Madrid, the worry was he only got better. He was always a threat. On form he was always a worry. The thing that made him even better was the amount of goals he started to score. Creatively he can always make a difference from anywhere on the pitch. When I think about the best goal he's ever scored, I can't narrow it down to just one.' The fact that a large portion of Real Madrid fans actively hate him has much to do with the threat he possesses. Secretly, they would love to him wearing the white of Madrid.

As for Barcelona fans, their devotion may be encapsulated in the words of Ernest Macià, a broadcaster for Catalunya Radio when he suggested: 'God may be Catalan?' When it became known that Messi's great grandmother was Catalan, everybody understood that something special was going on at their club. The best player ever had Catalan ancestors. The likes of Pelé, Maradona and Cruyff did not, and they seem to come short when compared to Messi, who has become an icon in a region of Spain that claims to be an independent state. He can easily be regarded as matching the height of genius of such as Antoni Gaudí or Salvador Dalí. Catalans often call him 'God'.

Messi has revealed that his best friend in the Barcelona dressing room is the outgoing Alves. He always maintained relationships with the Argentina footballers with whom he won Olympic Gold, specifically Sergio Agüero and Pablo Zabaleta. The fact that his partner is a childhood friend should give you a clue about who he trusts. He can sometimes spend several minutes texting or chatting with his friends in Rosario. He does not walk around with a particularly large entourage of friends in Barcelona, and in recent years has devoted most of his spare time to his family. Despite the tax fraud conviction of 2016, his father retains a massive interest in Team Messi.

It was his father, who was so convinced about his son's talent even when he was a young boy that he played hardball over negotiations on his early contracts. Maybe that explains the kind of footballer Messi has become, as he explained to *FourFourTwo* magazine. 'There are people who suggest that my way of playing football is innate. I do not know if this is the case. But it is true that I have a gambler's instinct. On the pitch I'm always looking to make the best move or the best decision, while trying not to do what the opponent expects me to do. When I feel the grass under my feet, I feel safe. I use the huge pressure to be better because pressure helps me to develop my skills.'

Behind every great man

Epilogue

I hate to have to break the news, but Lionel Messi cannot play forever. Certainly not as a professional, anyway. He has not made any noises about wanting to extend his football involvement beyond playing. So unless they change the laws of the game, it seems highly unlikely that he will reach the magical mark of one thousand goals. If he plays until he is thirty-five there is an outside chance he might get to eight hundred.

He has four Champions League medals. If he makes it a record five, he will probably have to share it with teammate Andrés Iniesta. The pair will also hope to take their tally of La Liga titles into double figures. But while Messi's teammate will always be a midfielder, where will Messi find himself in years to come? It seems logical, perhaps inevitable, that he will drift back to midfield. The acceleration required to take him into the final third of the pitch will ultimately disappear. There will also be a new generation of Messis coming through. Players who might convince the player that it is time to rethink where his talents are best utilised; it might even be that these up-and-coming stars who ultimately take his place are players he inspired.

That point in football history looks some way off. Messi has already had a long career, but advances in sport science and nutrition mean we should expect greater longevity from the world's greatest player. Could he come to England? Some say that day will certainly arrive; others say if he were to leave Barcelona, it would simply be to go back home to his first love, Newell's Old Boys.

‘

THERE ARE THREE OR FOUR IMPORTANT THINGS IN LIFE: BOOKS, FRIENDS, WOMEN... AND MESSI.

’

António Lobo Antunes – Portuguese writer

It was when I first watched Messi, in the flesh, that I finally understood his true genius. Seeing the mastery with which he drifts from the wings to the middle – using his height and frame to manoeuvre around his opponents with the same enthusiasm of his childhood days. Some coaches like to define football by players and their positions, for example, is a player a striker or a 'number 10'. Messi has proved to be both and neither. He plays his own game and dares you to define him. Taking the ball from the goalkeeper or loitering outside the penalty box is not an indication of how the game is going as much as it says where he feels he can create danger on the day. For the one thing he has always had, above and beyond any other current player, is his football brain. The weapon that allows him to be at the start, middle or end of moves. It is like he has the most sophisticated computer inside that cranium that allows him to make decisions on the pitch that you can only understand after the ball hits the net. It is this that makes him endlessly fascinating to watch, and it is this that allows him to continue to be the elite of the elite. Describing him as a playmaker or forward does not do justice to him. He is Lionel Messi, the best player in the world. Just call him that.

Picture and Data Credits

Data Credits
Where applicable, data is correct up until the end of 2015–16 season, unless otherwise stated. With special thanks to Opta for their help and expertise.

Data provided by Opta – www.optasports.com
22-23, 40, 41, 70-71, 74-75, 82-83, 118-119, 124-125, 138, 140-141, 148-149, 156, 157, 178, 179.

Bibliography

Websites in alphabetical order:

as.com

barcablaugranes.com

bbc.co.uk

bleacherreport.com

cbssports.com

dailymail.co.uk

defendingwiththeball.wordpress.com

earnthenecklace.com

eurosport.co.uk

fcbarcelona.com

fieldoo.com

fifa.com

fourfourtwo.com

givemesport.com

goal.com

guardian.com

independent.co.uk

manchestereveningnews.co.uk

marca.com

mensfitnessmagazine.com.au

messinews.net

nytimes.com

outsideoftheboot.com

quora.com

skysports.com

slate.com

soccerlens.com

sport-english.com

sport-magazine.co.uk

tattoodo.com

telegraph.co.uk

thefalse9.com

totalsportek.com

uefa.com

yahoo.com

zonalmarking.net

Acknowledgements

Daunting is how I would describe being asked to write a book about the greatest footballer to ever live. Thank you, in no particular order to Rob Palmer, Steve McManaman, Trevor Sinclair, Reshmin Chowdhury, Ernest Macià, Diego Jokas, Sid Lowe and Marcela Mora y Araujo. There were others who were happy to speak to me, but on the condition of anonymity. As the bibliography will testify, there were many articles that helped me put this journey in perspective. I am also thankful for having the good sense to read *Messi* by Guillem Balague, Graham Hunter's *Barça: The Making of the Greatest Team in the World*, and for a little inspiration, *Living on the Volcano* by Michael Calvin.

May I also add to that list the many people I have worked with on BBC World TV and BBC World Service. Adnan Nawaz and Francis Collings have helped give me a particular insight into the ways that football works in different countries, but there were many others. Thank you as well to Opta for their painstaking research into the goals, assists, heat maps and other statistics that I am only just finding out about now!

Lucy Warburton at Aurum came to me about two years ago with this project and her constant reassurance and reminders of what we need to make it work have been invaluable. And those thanks should be extended to Martin Smith and Alison Anderson for the painstaking copy-editing and proof-reading. Alison, you are great, even if you are older than me.

As always, you need an understanding family to be able to devote endless hours to something they cannot see. Laura, thank you for being intelligent, selfless and beautiful. Raf – you are cut from the same jib. And a special mention for my youngest, who helped me when the book was still in its infancy, with ideas for chapters. He also took over the keyboard when his old man's fingers were a little sore. Thank you, Bulse.

Eleven days before I committed to this book, my mother left this world. I had reservations about accepting the challenge, but every time I thought about doing something else, words from somewhere else filled my head. 'Of course, you have to do it!' she would have said. She grew me, raised me and then she made me. Thanks, Mum. For everything.

Index

A

Abidal, Éric 72
AC Milan 66, 100, 208, 238
Adidas 227
Adriano 138
Agostino, Homero de 48
Agüero, Sergio 106, 111, 137, 187, 203, 245
Alba, Jordi 138, 154, 175, 184, 193
Albacete 18
Albiol, Raúl 67
Allegri, Massimo 176
Almería 81
Almunia, Manuel 72
Alonso, Xabi 66, 83, 238
Alves, Dani 57, 74, 82, 138, 155, 172, 176, *182*, 238, 245
Anderson 64, 162, 167
Anello, Gabriel 107
Antunes, Antonio Lobo 249
Argentina (national team) 2, 9, *9*, *13*, 16, 19, 20, *20*, 25–7, 29, 33, 38, 44, 45, 48, 51, 60, 101, *102–3*, *104*, 106–25, *109*, *112*, *114*, *121*, 123, 130, 137, 139, 186, 187, *194*, *195*, 202, 215, 218–19, *220–1*, 222, *231*, 245
    Copa América and see Copa América
    Messi as all-time leading scorer 107
    Messi as world's best player and 218–19
    Messi caps 107
    Messi debut 25–6, 107
    Messi hat-tricks 29, *29*
    Messi retirement 106, 107, 123, 202
    World Cup and see World Cup
Arsenal 19, 25, 67, 72, 132, 189, 192, 214, 243
AS 44
Athletic Bilbao 64, 130, 155, 185, 209
Atlético Madrid 47, 67, 80, 139, 154–5, 175, 190, 192, 193, 244
Ayala, Roberto 26, 45

B

Bale, Gareth 12, *12*, 43, *43*, 82, 137, 141
Ballon d'Or 19, 56, 72–3, 92, 97, 99, 139, 147, 175, *181*, *182*, 188–9, *210–11*, *212*, 214, 216
Banega, Éver 106, 111
Barcelona 4, 14, 30–1, *32*, 37, 42, 46, 53, 54, 58, 63, 65, 68, 76–7, 78, 86, 90, *126–7*, *128*, *133*, *136*, *142–3*, *144*, *150–1*, *153*, *158–9*, *160*, *163*, *164–5*, *168*, 176, *191*, *196*, *198*, *200*, 226, *242*, *246–7*
    Champions League and see Champions League
    Copa del Rey and see Copa del Rey
    La Liga and see La Liga
    Messi debut for senior side 4, *4*, 10
    Messi departure from, rumours of 137, 187
    Messi first goal for 18–19
    Messi first signs contract with 3, 8, 10
    Messi signs first professional contract for 19
    Messi trial for 6
    MSN (Messi, Suárez, Neymar) and 147–8, 149, 152, 174, 177, 187, 190, 192, 202, 240

tiki-taka and 56, 154
    win ratio with Messi starting 80, *80*, 81, *81*
    youth sides, Messi in 10
Bartomeu, Josep 187
Basten, Marco van 10, 48
Batista, Sergio 111, 113
Batistuta, Gabriel 123
Bayer Leverkusen 131, 156, 157, 214
Bayern Munich 94, 130, 131, 132, 135, 138, 149, 152, 217, 239
Beckham, David 34, 94, 100, 118
Begiristain, Txiki 44, 187
Belgium 38, 120
Benítez, Rafael 188, 238
Benzema, Karim 66, 83, 93, 192
Berbatov, Dimitar 167
Bergkamp, Dennis 10
Best, George 24, 62
Beto 185
Boateng, Jérôme 152
Borussia Dortmund 135
Brau, Juanjo 59
Brazil 29, 45, 50, 107, 115, 116, 118, 120, 122, 137, 208, 218
Bryant, Kobe 225, 228
Buffon, Gianluigi 175, 176, 177
Busquets, Sergio 57, 59, 110, 162, 176, 177, 184

C

Cambiasso, Esteban 111
Cannavaro, Fabio 61, 62
Capello, Fabio 17, 19, 24, 36
Carrick, Michael 64, 167, 169
Casillas, Iker 35, 36, 61, 62, 67, 76, 81, 82, 85, 131
Cate, Henk ten 137
Cech, Petr 189
Celta Vigo 185, 190
Champions League 94, 186, 248
    2001–2 214
    2005–6 19, 24, 25, 189
    2006–7 35
    2007–8 47, 48–9, 227
    2008–9 59, 62, 64–5, 66, 148–9, 158–9, 162–3, *163*, 164–5, 166
    2009–10 67, 72
    2010–11 84, 85, 113, 168–9, 172–4, 178, 238
    2011–12 130, 131, 132, 155, 156, 157
    2012–13 134–5
    2013–14 139
    2014–15 *142–3*, *144*, 147, 149, *150–1*, 152, *153*, 154–5, 174–7, 176, 179, 217
    2015–16 184, 185, 187, 188, 189, 190, 192, 193, 243, 244
    Messi and Ronaldo record in 97
    Messi average goal times 22, *23*
    Messi average tackles made per game 82–3
    Messi coverage in 178, *179*
    Messi goalscoring and assist record in 152, 156, *170*, *171*
    Messi hat-tricks 29, *29*
    Messi playing for Enrique in 241
    Messi predicted goals in *220–1*

Messi results under Guardiola in 69
Messi UEFA best goal in, 2014–15 217
Chelsea 24, 25, 34, 48, 62, 64, 130, 146, 184, 238
Chile 106, 123, 209
Chivu, Cristian 72
Clichy, Gaël 72
Club World Cup 69, 97, 186, 241
    2009 66
    2012 130
    2015 189
Copa América 186, 193, 202
    1993 106
    2007 45, 107
    2008 106
    2011 111, 113, 114–15, 132
    2015 123, 155
    2016 106, 107, 123, 193
Copa del Rey 69, 97, 130, 216, 241
    2006–7 38–9, 44–5
    2007–8 49
    2008–9 59, 64, 66
    2010–11 84
    2011–12 130, 208
    2012–13 209
    2014–15 147, 155
    2015–16 190, 193, 202
Crespo, Hernán 26
Cruyff, Johan 21, *21*, 56, 60, 62, 91, 98, 190, 206, 239, 240, 245

D

debuts, professional 20, *20*, 21, *21*
Deco 10, 24, 26, *30*, 44, 49
Del Piero, Alessandro 202
Demichellis, Martin 115
Dí Maria, Angel 106, 115, 120
di Stéfano, Alfredo 26, 28, 98
Djokovic, Novak 12, *12*, 228
Drenthe, Royston 61
dribbling:
    dribble rates 140
    fastest dribblers 141
Drogba, Didier 38

E

El Clásico *90*, 93
    2008–9 61–2
    2010–11 76–7, 78, 79–85, 95
    2014–15 147
    2015–16 187–8, 192
    Messi goalscoring record 244
El Pais 65
Enrique, Luis 93, 94, 136, 139, 147, 183, 187, 239, 240, 241, 242, 243
Espanyol 10, 80, 154, 208, 244
Essien, Michael 62
Eto, Samuel 18, 24, 35, 36, 47, 49, 56, 57, 61, 64, 66, 71, 73, 113, 163, 167, 169, 237, 239
European Championships 45, 122
    2000 214
    2008 111
    2012 167
European Cup 162, 192
    1991–92 162, 185
European Super Cup:
    2009 66
    2015 184–5
Everton 192
Evra, Patrice 64, 146, 167, 172–3, 175–6

F

Fàbregas, Cesc 8, 132, 146
Federer, Roger 227, 229
Ferdinand, Rio 64, 162, *163*, 164, 173

Ferguson, Sir Alex 64, 93, 94, 167, 173, 174, *182*, 192, 238
FIFA U20 World Cup: 2005 9
FIFA World Player of the Year 73, *210–11*, *212*, 214
Figo, Luís 19, 79
FourFourTwo 245

G

Gago, Fernando 106
Germany 26, 27, 106, 107, 110, 111, 115, 116, 117, 118, 119, 120, 122, 124, 125, 131, 135, 209, 219
Getafe 38–9, 44–5, 208
Giggs, Ryan 64, 83, 162, 169
Glasgow Rangers 11
Gómez, Mario 29, 135
Gonzalez, Raul 79
Götze, Mario 122
Granada 189, 208
Grandoli 5
Guardian 35
Guardiola, Pep 49, 52, 54, 55, 56, 57, 58, 59, 60, 63, 66, 68, 69, 80, 105, 107, 110, 130, 131, 132, 136, 138, 145, 149, 152–3, 169, 173, 174, 177, 187, 238, 239–40, 243
Gudjohnsen, Eidur 18
Gullit, Ruud 10, 213
Guttmann, Béla 80

H

Hä ler, Thomas 119
Heinze, Gabriel 45, 61, 62
Helguera, Iván 36
Henry, Thierry 38, 45, 47, 56, 57, 61, 169, 239
Hércules 80
Higuaín, Gonzalo 61, 106, 115, 120
Hleb, Alexander 57
Holland 27, 120
Horno, Asier del 24
Hory, Elmyr 44

I

Ibrahimović, Zlatan 66, 67, 81, 86, 87, 100, 113, 148, 203, 226
Ighalo, Odion 136
Iniesta, André 11, 25, 56, 58, 64, 73, 75, 82, 110, 131, 167, 172, 175, 176, 177, 187, 218, 238, 239, 248
Inter Milan 19, 66, 72, 80

J

James, LeBron 13, *13*, 227, 229, 232
Juventus 19, *150–1*, 155, 174–7, *176*, 202, 214

K

Kaka 38, 66
Keane, Roy 201
Keita, Seydou 57
Kempes, Mario 122
Klopp, Jürgen 135
Klose, Miroslav 116–17
Koeman, Ronald 162, 185
Krkic, Bojan 64

L

La Liga:
    2004–5 18
    2005–6 24
    2006–7 35–6
    2007–8 45, 47, 48, 49
    2008–9 56, 57, 59, 61–2
    2009–10 66–7
    2010–11 80, 81, 113
    2011–12 130, 134, 155, 156
    2012–13 134, 135–6
    2013–14 137, 138, 139
    2014–15 147–9, 154, 155

2015–16 74–5, 136, 138, 185, 189–90, 192–3
fouls against Messi, 2015–16 136
Messi and Ronaldo record in 97
Messi average goal time in 22, 23
Messi goalscoring record in 206
Messi hat-tricks in 28, 28, 130, 189–90
Messi most goals scored in calendar year (2012) and 208, 209
Messi playing for Enrique in 241
Messi results under Guardiola in 69
Messi titles/trophies 217, 248
Lacueva, Joan 8
Laporta, Joan 19
Larsson, Henrik 25
Lato, Gregorz 119
Lavezzi, Ezequiel 106, 111
Lawton, James 24
Leeds United 192
Lineker, Gary 213, 214
Littbarski, Pierre 119
Liverpool 80, 146, 175, 184, 185, 192, 238
Lowe, Sid 35, 131

M

Manchester City 80, 98, 137, 152–3, 187
Manchester United 48–9, 64–5, 80, 93–4, 146, 162–3, 163, 164–5,
166–7, 168–9,
168, 172–3, 175, 192, 238
Maradona, Diego 2, 26, 33, 34, 35, 38, 39, 44, 62, 98, 103, 107–8,
109, 110, 111, 113,
119, 120, 194, 195, 201, 203, 215, 218, 245
Marchisio, Claudio 176
Martino, Gerardo 122–3, 136, 138, 139
Mascherano, Javier 45, 106, 108, 111, 115, 120, 193
Materazzi, Marco 214
Mathieu, Jérémy 154
McLeish, Alex 11
McLeish, Jon 11
McManaman, Steve 94
Menotti, Cesar Luis 60, 139
Mercado, Gabriel 107
Messi, Jorge (father) 5, 6, 8, 10, 123, 230, 245
Messi, Lionel:
    appearance/style 198, 202
    appearances for club and nation compared 196, 197
    Argentina and (international career) see Argentina
    assists, 2015–16 season 138
    Barcelona career see Barcelona
    as best player in the world 19, 34, 56, 72–3, 92–3, 94, 106, 113,
    120, 169, 177, 213, 214–19, 240
    birth 2
    as captain 219
    Catalans and 245
    Champions League and see Champions League
    childhood 2, 3, 5, 6, 7
    children and girlfriend 230
    cup competitions and see under individual cup competition name
    diet and lifestyle 59
    dribble rate 140
    early years 1–11
    earnings in comparison to celebrities 232–3
    earnings in comparison to other sportsmen 228–9
    end of career 248
    endorsements 230–1
    family 2, 5, 35–6
    fastest dribblers and 141
    fouls against 24, 136
    free kicks 67, 87, 100, 101, 122, 130, 134, 152, 154, 162, 184–5
    goal time, average 22, 22, 23
    goals at Nou Camp 216
    goalscoring record 22, 23, 24, 57, 130–1, 134, 137, 147–8, 174–5,
    192–3, 204, 205, 206, 208, 209, 216, 220–1, 238, 248
    growth hormone deficiency/treatment 5–6, 8
hat-tricks, career 29, 29, 130–1

hat-tricks, Champions League 29, 29, 131
hat-tricks, La Liga 28, 28, 130, 189–90
    hatred of losing 8
    height and weight compared to other top sportsmen 12, 12, 13
    highest career goals record compared to other football greats 203
    injuries 25, 47–8, 59–60, 138, 185–6, 187–8, 193, 218
    La Liga and see La Liga
    'La Pulga'/'The Flea' nickname 2
    Maradona and see Maradona
    metatarsal injury, 2006–7 34–5
    most goals in a season 204, 205
    most goals scored in calendar year 208, 209
    penalties scored and missed 112, 112
    percentage of touches, Champions League, 2009 148–9
    personal trophies 217
    personal wealth 227, 230
pitch coverage and movement 40, 40, 41
player salaries and 226
playing for Enrique 241
playing style and injury 59–60
    position on pitch 24, 56, 59, 62, 82, 92, 131, 132, 147–8, 169,
    184, 207, 240, 248, 249
post-match comments 24
predicted goals if continues to 35 220–1
professional debuts 20, 20, 21, 21
Real Madrid attempt to sign 244
results under management of Pep Guardiola 68, 69
Ronaldo, record versus 96, 97
Ronaldo in El Clásico, record versus 95
school 5
small stature 2, 5–6, 8, 25
sponsorship contracts 227
sprint speed in comparison with other forward players 42, 42, 43
    tackles made per game in Champions League, average 82–3, 82–3
tattoos 230
tax fraud investigation 139, 230, 245
use of body to score goals 86, 86, 87
value 19
wages 226, 227, 228–9, 230
who does Messi help score the most? 70, 70–1
who helps Messi score the most? 74, 74–5
World Cup and see World Cup
Messi, Mateo (son) 230
Messi, Thiago (son) 230, 231
Mexico 27, 45, 51, 110
Minguella, Josep Maria 6, 10
Morata, Alvaro 177
Motta, Thiago 24
Mourinho, José 72, 80, 82, 84
MSN (Messi, Suárez, Neymar) 147–8, 149, 152, 174, 177, 187, 190,
192, 202, 240
Müller, Gerd 116–17, 131–2
Müller, Thomas 118, 135

N

Neuer, Manuel 120, 122, 149, 152
Neville, Gary 94, 190
Newell's Old Boys 107, 123, 136, 231, 248
Neymar 42, 42, 70, 93, 137, 146–7, 148, 152, 155, 174, 175, 176,
177, 184, 187,
188, 189, 190, 193, 202, 206, 218, 240, 243
Nigeria 106, 110
Numancia 56

O

O'Shea, John 167
Olympics: 2008 (Beijing) 9, 106, 186, 245
Otamendi, Nicolás 106
Özil, Mesut 83, 92

P

Palmer, Rob 18–19
Paris Saint-Germain 135, 147

Park Ji-sung 163, 166, 167, 169
Pedro 66, 67, 70, 72, 74, 82, 85, 113, 155, 169, 184
Pékerman, José 26, 27, 107
Pelé 20, *20*, 29, 116–17, 118, 120, 137, 177, *182*, 190, 196–7, 203, 213, 215, 218, 245
Pepe 84
Peru 45
Piqué, Gerard 8, 57, 192
Pirlo, Andrea 176
Pogba, Paul 176
Premier League 11, 64, 94, 98, 136, 137, 146, 175, 192, 238
Puyol, Carlos 57, 61, 146

R

Racing Santander 56
Rakitic, Ivan 153, 155, 175
Ramos, Juande 61
Ramos, Sergio 36, 61, 83, 141, 192
Raúl 61, 79
Real Madrid 8, *12*, 15, 18, *21*, 29, 34, 35–6, 38, 43, 48, 49, 61–2, 64, 66–7, 72, 76–7, 79–85, 90–1, 91, 92, 94, 96, 100, 101, 130, 131, 135, 137, 139, 146, 147, 154, 175, 184, 187–8, 190, 192, 193, *197*, 204, 209, 214, 244
Real Sociedad 147
Relaño, Alfredo 44
Rexach, Charly 6, 8, 10
Ribéry, Franck 94, 141
Rijkaard, Frank 10, 18, 34, 47–8, 49, 56
Riquelme, Juan Román 26, 45, 108
River Plate 6, 8, 189
Robben, Arjen 48, 120, 135
Roccuzzo, Antonella 230
Rodríguez, James 93
Roma 188
Romario 203
Ronaldinho *14–15*, 18, 19, 24, 34, 35, 36, 47, 49, 214
Ronaldo, Cristiano 12, *12*, 19, 21, *21*, 28, 29, 38, 43, 64, 65, 66, 73, 79, 81, 82, 83, 84, *88*, 89, 90–101, 93, 99, 115–16, 123, 132, 141, 147, 152, 154, 162, 166, 167, 168, 175, 184, 185, 188, 192, 193, 196–7, 201, 203, 204–5, 206, 215, 226, 227, 229, 233
Ronaldo, Luís Nazário 203
Rooney, Wayne 13, *13*, 21, *21*, 42, *42*, 64, 82, 141, 162, 172, 196–7, *196*, 203, 213
Rosario, Argentina 2, 18, 123, 132, 162, 227, 229, 244, 245

S

Sabella, Alejandro 105, 114, *114*, 115
Sacchi, Arrigo 66
Sampdoria 162
Sánchez, Alexis 146
Sánchez, Oswaldo 45
Santos 137
Scholes, Paul 49, 162
Schuster, Bernd 61
Schweinsteiger, Bastian 118
Scottish Premier League 11
Serbia 26, 27, 107
Sevilla 36, 184–5, 190, 193, 208, 228
Shearer, Alan 196–7, *196*
Simeone, Diego 139, 154
Sinclair, Trevor 98
Sky Sports 18, 72
Spain 111, 115, 137
Spanish Super Cup 97, 216, 219
    2006 34
    2009 66
    2012 130
    2015 185
Steckelmacher, Hugo 47, 48
Stegen, Marc-André ter 152

Stoichkov, Hristo 161
Suárez, Luis 70, 71, 93, 138, 146, 147, 148, 152, 155, 174, 175–6, 177, 184, 187, 188, 189, 190, 193, 202, 203, 204–5, 206, 207, 218, 240, 243
Switzerland 29, 115, 120, 208

T

Tevez, Carlos 64, 106, 108, 111, 167, 176
tiki-taka 56, 154
Toquero, Gaizka 64
Totti, Francesco 118
Touré, Yaya 45, 64
Tyldesley, Clive 169

U

Unicef 230
Uruguay 50, 106, 113, 146, 174, 175, 184, 188, 189, 202, 209, 220

V

Valdés, Víctor 146
Valencia 43, 64, 67, 81, 114, 189–90, 192–3, 208
Valencia, Antonio 43, *43*, 141, 172, 173
van der Sar, Edwin 162, 163, *164*–5, 167, 169, 173
Vermaelen, Thomas 190
Verón, Juan Sebastián 19
Vickery, Tim 26
Vidić, Nemanja 64, 162, 173
Vilanova, Tito 131, 135, 136, 137
Villa, David 71, 81, 82, 113, 138, 148, 169, 172, 173, 218

W

Wenger, Arsène 67, 72, 192, 214
Woods, Tiger 130, 227, 228
World Cup 122, 186
    1958 218
    1970 190, 218
    1978 2, 122
    1986 2, 26, 38, 39, 215
    1990 2
    1998 214
    2002 98
    2006 25, 26–7, 107, 214
    2010 108, 110, 111, 218
    2014 106, 115, 120, *121*, 122, 123, 124–5, 135, 146, 218–19
    2018 202, 207
    assists 118–19
    debuts 20, 21
    goals 9, 115–16
Messi heat map, 2014 124–5
    red cards 50, 51
    youngest scorer 26, 27

X

Xavi 56, 61–2, 67, 72, 73, 75, 82, 110, 131, 146, 147, 167, 172, 174, 218, 238–9

Z

Zabaleta, Pablo 106, 137, 187, 245
Zanetti, Javier 72
Zidane, Zinedine 11, 34, 79, 190, 192, 214, 215

Quarto is the authority on a wide range of topics
Quarto educates, entertains and enriches the lives of
our readers – enthusiasts and lovers of hands-on living.
www.QuartoKnows.com

First published in Great Britain
2017 by Aurum Press Ltd
74–77 White Lion Street
Islington
London N1 9PF

A catalogue record for this book is available from the British Library.

ISBN 978 1 78131 607 8

Ebook ISBN 978 1 78131 698 6

10 9 8 7 6 5 4 3 2 1

2021 2020 2019 2018 2017

Design and graphics: Founded / founded.design

Printed in China